Take charge of your health

Most of us have depended on doctors and modern medicine to heal our ills and keep us healthy. Certainly the professionals and life-saving pharmaceuticals have done wonders in keeping us alive and kicking. But during the last half-century, a good number of people have sought to live healthier lives by taking more responsibility for, and control of, their well-being with better nutrition, exercise, and hygiene.

Now Nancy Anna Blitz, a nurse for four decades and a Reiki Master for two decades, has taken the vital marriage of Western medicine and Eastern energy practices to a new level. In *Ésprit with SoZoKi / A Practitioner's Manual,* she explains how we can help ourselves have healthier bodies and minds.

Ésprit with *SoZoKi*

A Practitioner's Manual

Ésprit with *SoZoKi*

A Practitioner's Manual

by Nancy Anna Blitz

Charlottesville, Virginia
Carmel, California

May 2021

Ésprit with SoZoKi / A Practitioner's Manual is a companion to my book *SoZoKi/Creation's Energy*, which I wrote to promote your development of a self-energy practice. All of the information in this book is accurate, much of it based on my personal experience and observation.

The drawings in these pages are by the author.

Ésprit with *SoZoKi*

A Practitioner's Manual

Copyright © 2021 by Nancy Anna Blitz

No part of this book may be reproduced or transmitted in any form or by any means, electronic or mechanical, including photocopying, recording, or by any information storage and retrieval system, without permission in writing from the publisher. For information about the author, please visit her site at SoZoKi.com.

ISBN: 978-1-7349057-8-6

Ésprit with SoZoKi

Table of Contents

Dedication .... - i -

Introduction .... - iii -

Chakras & SoZoKi .... - 1 -

2 - Root Chakra (First) .... - 6 -

3 - Sacral Chakra (Second) .... - 12 -

4 - Solar Plexus Chakra (Third) .... - 18 -

5 - Heart Chakra (Fourth) .... - 24 -

6 - Throat Chakra (Fifth) .... - 31 -

7 - Third Eye Chakra (Sixth) .... - 38 -

8 - Crown Chakra (Seventh) .... - 45 -

9 - SoZoKi Self-Practice .... - 54 -
    Starting & Ending Each Day .... - 54 -
    Fresh New Beginnings .... - 57 -
    Creating Your Space .... - 59 -
    Define Your Rituals .... - 61 -
    Successful Meditation .... - 67 -

Ésprit with SoZoKi

Reinforce Patterns . . . . - 69 -
Removing Caustic Circumstances & People . - 72 -
Inviting Energy of the Spirit. . . . . - 75 -
The Reiki Ideals . . . . - 79 -
The Great Invocation. . . . . - 79 -
Shaman White Light of Protection Prayer - 80 -
The Shaman's Prayer. . . . . - 81 -
Feet & Hand Chakras . . . . - 82 -

10 - Hand Positions . . . . - 88 -

11 - Ésprit Energy Meditations . . . . - 104 -
    Non-Guided Meditation . . . . - 104 -
    Guided Ésprit Meditation . . . . - 106 -

To Your Good Health . . . . - 114 -

Test Questions . . . . - 115 -

Test Answers. . . . . - 150 -

Glossary. . . . . - 151 -

Endnotes . . . . - 157 -

About the Author. . . . . - 166 -

Ésprit with SoZoKi

Dedication

This book is dedicated to the following nurses:

Jenelle Blitz, RN
Ernestine Brown, RN
Barb Florence, RN
Ruth Graves, RN
Christie McGuire, RN
Rhonda Newby, RN

Courageous Women, Excellent Nurses and each an Amazing She-ro!

Thank you for your exceptional service to, and influence on, humanity!

Ésprit with SoZoKi

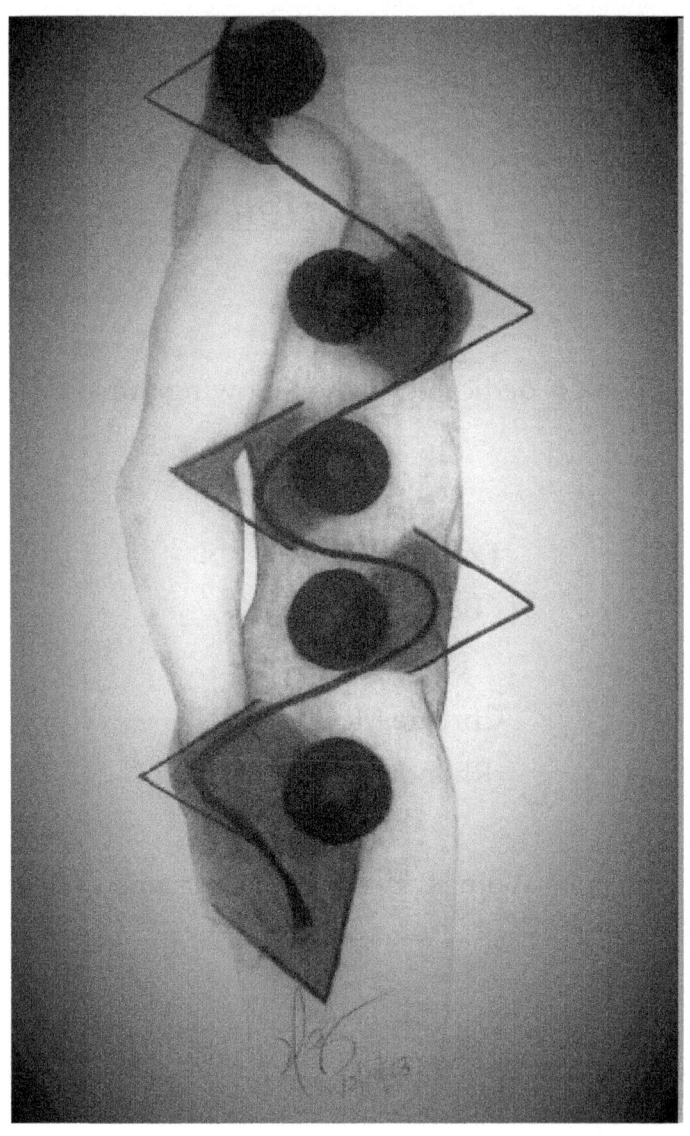

"SoZoKi Flows" (2016)

Ésprit with SoZoKi

Introduction

Ésprit with SoZoKi / A Practitioner's Manual is a companion to my book *SoZoKi/Creation's Energy*, which I wrote to promote your development of a self-energy practice. To live your best life, your *Ésprit with SoZoKi* practice helps you refine the art of inviting energy of the Spirit into your life. I do not mind sharing my age ... rather I am proud I have made it this far: 64 years young! I have concluded most people think people my age should not have the life energy I possess. So many believe or witness people my age slowing down, not speeding up. People far younger act far older, and I am not referring to maturity or emotional intelligence. Again and again, I hear, "I wish I had your energy!" from people many years younger. Sooo, I am sharing what I've discovered -- the source of my energy -- and this program that I developed for you to feel younger, too.

You have probably heard of Reiki (pronounced ray-key). Reiki healing is a hands-on or hands-hovering practice using Universal Energy to assist in the resolution of a patient's physical and/or emotional issues. Establishing a Reiki practice

Ésprit with SoZoKi

requires attending an 8-hour class for each of three levels of practice: Reiki I, II and Master Certificates, with a fee charged for each level of education. A Reiki Master for years now, I believe that the practice can be taken to a new level, moving past the original structure of Reiki, to empower the individual to develop an energy self-practice. *SoZoKi* (pronounced so-zo-key) is the word I created for this next step in the energy healing arts that focuses on our chakra system. By adding two Japanese words together to create one: SoZo meaning Creation and Ki meaning energy. In these pages, I outline what *SoZoKi* is, how it works, and how you can apply it to your own needs. Share your experience so that you can show friends and family how they, too, can relieve "dis-ease" -- both physical and emotional -- for themselves.

When I began learning about Reiki, I held an Associate's Degree in Nursing (ADN), and had been a registered nurse for more than 15 years. I had specialized in operating room nursing. My first introduction came from a mother and daughter-in-law team who had no medical background and were offering their first time teaching of the class. I was a great student to have as I had many questions about the information they shared. At the end of the day, I was questioning myself about the limitations of what I had believed as a nurse scientist for more than a decade.

Ésprit with SoZoKi

It was difficult for me to accept that an energy practice could honestly have an impact on health, be it physical or emotional. I practiced on the fly on my fellow nurses and surgeons who vocalized an interest in trying Reiki. My offerings were not traditional sessions lasting 40 or 50 minutes, but more of an acute care offering of 5 to 10 minutes, wherever we were in the operating rooms.

I spent years reading and reviewing the available literature, and from my studies began to put together a much larger understanding of the chakra system's functionality and impact on health. From this focused exploration of all the elements of energy healing, I began to develop the concept that anyone can and should access Creation's Energy. At the same time, I added Bachelor (BSN) and Master (MSN) degrees to my formal education. But my deeper interest was in developing what has been named *Ésprit with SoZoKi*, to assist you on your path to a better understanding of our human experience and providing you with the capacity to help yourself heal.

This is what you will discover:

- How the chakra system manages your health.

- What are the multifunctional aspects of each chakra and methods to increase energy flow.

Ésprit with SoZoKi

- Which organs are associated with each chakra and how they are affected by different health practices.

- How you can develop your own individual *SoZoKi* practice.

When you have absorbed the information in these pages pertaining to your ethereal energy body -- the chakra system -- and how you can optimize its functioning, you will be able to custom develop an energy healing self-practice that supports and maintains your physical and emotional well-being.

At the end of the text, there are 94 questions to help you confirm that you have learned the essence of the information you will want to know. Don't worry about being graded. It's an open book test with the answers in the next section so that you can make sure not only that you get the answers right, but also that you understand how you can heal yourself and fully share your wisdom with others.

Ésprit with SoZoKi

1 - Chakras & SoZoKi

Its familiar name is *chakra*. Also known as an energy wheel. It is a swirling conical vortex in the body's *ethereal energy field*. The ethereal energy field is part of the energy aura that each human produces, and is the layer that lies closest to the physical body.

There are seven major chakras, each located where 21 lines of meridian, or energy highways, intersect. Located just below the perineum, the area between the legs where they join the torso is the location of the first chakra. The seventh is located just above the head, and in between the two lie the other five chakras. (There are additional minor chakras located where lines of a lessor number of energy highways throughout the body cross, but here we will only discuss the seven majors).

To best understand, the chakras are a multi-dimensional system, and the interconnectedness of this system is an essential part of its nature. Each chakra, each energy vortex, supplies energy to the

Ésprit with SoZoKi

local anatomical organs. When healthy and functioning without blocks, the chakras also promote inspiration and intuition as well as influence, judgments, and opinions. They also affect how we communicate with others, and how we perceive our place in Creation. Attunement to our soul or spirit is colored by the vitality of our chakras.

Our ethereal energy system is strongly associated with our physiological organs and circulation. As we come to understand the functions of the chakras, we will see each is identified with both traditionally feminine and masculine tendencies. I will explain each chakra's function for you to diagnose or understand how and why a chakra may not be functioning at its fullest and what the effects can be on your energy system. It's important to know what is wrong because sub-par function can not only diminish energy, but can also impact our consciousness, our psyche, and the presence of disease in the physical body. You will learn as well ways to open chakras that are blocked.

While I offer this information to assist you in enhancing and safeguarding your spiritual, emotional and physical well-being, you must always avail yourself of different health care systems -- e.g., both Eastern and Western approaches to good health -- and not throw either away when you are in need. The fact is that they

Ésprit with SoZoKi

work best in conjunction. So never decide to close your mind to visiting your medical (MD) or osteopathic (DO) doctor. Such a stance can jeopardize your health and diminish your ability to recover from injury or illness.

Also, I would advise that it is imperative that you have a strong relationship with your pharmacist. If you are taking supplements, you will want to be sure that they don't react negatively with or negate the effectiveness of prescribed Western medications. Similarly, if you see a naturopath, you also need to see a medical doctor, a physician's assistant, or a nurse practitioner. If you see a chiropractor, it should be in conjunction with your primary care physician, and your orthopedic or neurosurgical specialist if you have been referred to one.

A medical exam is essential to ensuring that nothing is missed in diagnosing a condition. You want to make sure that an advancement of symptoms won't result in an untreatable terminal disease. Once cleared by an MD or DO, you can seek the help of an alternative/supplemental provider. And it might be you find that you don't need to see the medical doctor again for the particular disorder. As a registered nurse, I have seen mistakes on both "sides" of the health care spectrum. That's why I so strongly believe that those who begin their *SoZoKi* self-practice commit

Ésprit with SoZoKi

to the balanced Eastern-Western approach to good health care.

* * * * *

In a *SoZoKi* self-practice, we request energy from Creation to increase our own natural flow. There are many names for the energy that is accessed in this practice. Divine Design, Creation, God, and E Pluribus Unum are just some of the names. However, for the purposes of this manual, I'm referring to the energy as that of *Creation*. It is important to note here that a *SoZoKi* practice does not replace any religious faith. You can be of any faith or of none and still engage the *Ésprit with SoZoKi* without challenging any of your spiritual beliefs. In addition, it is for this reason that someone of any belief or a skeptic can successfully receive and benefit from Creation's energy.

The fundamental ideological difference between Reiki and *SoZoKi* is that while only those attuned through ritual by a master can access the limited universe energy (Reiki), anyone who is aware and has desire can access unlimited Creation Energy (*SoZoKi*). This is our attachment of spirit or soul to the natural energy flow; not at the behest of an anointed human. *SoZoKi* sustains all life on earth be it plant, insect, animal, and human. *SoZoKi* is not a conscious effort to pull earth or universe energy, but rather a practice to support a continuous subconscious flow of energy into our ethereal

Ésprit with SoZoKi

body. While naturally occurring energy flow can be subconsciously diminished or blocked, more importantly it can be consciously requested to increase. Understanding that energy is condensed to form mass -- so that our spirit can have this earthly experience -- gives birth to the ideal that human life is the process of evolution from human to spiritual consciousness.

2 - Root Chakra (First)

The first chakra is known as the Root. Located just below the perineum, the space between the anus and genitals, it connects to the lowest bone in the spine called the coccyx. It is primarily through this chakra that Creation Energy enters the human body's ethereal system. The Root Chakra has a positive polarity, pushing energy into the ethereal body and then upward into the second or the Sacral Chakra.

The prime functions of the Root Chakra are grounding, security, and survival. Primal energy, along with the impulse toward taking care of self and others, are fundamental (Root) functions. When the Root is closed, we shut ourselves off to inspired thought, and experience fear, anxiety, and depression. In America, our society is heavily focused on Western philosophies and religious practices, which are often unaccepting of diversity, including Eastern philosophies and practices. The Divine principle or goal for this chakra is to maintain simplicity and stability, as well as provide

Ésprit with SoZoKi

self-preservation with primal instincts while promoting awakening of consciousness from human to spirit. This is hardly what children in this country will hear from their parents or their school teachers, let alone their religious leaders.

We can see the impact of a closed Root Chakra in our country. Americans have a high rate of occurrence of infertility, elimination complications, and psychosocial disorders. [1.] 5The prevalence of a dog-eat-dog mentality in a concrete jungle is evidence of a society suffering from a dis-attachment of our spirit to *SoZoKi*. It is through the Root Chakra that inspired thought enters into our human consciousness, rather than the popular belief of initiation in the brain.

> Our brain has a different function. It is the relay center for our nervous system, be it action, reaction, or thought. Consider that we can act to prevent injury or we can react to injury with the experience of pain. We can also respond to a thought and ultimately remove from the harmful stimuli.
>
> When injury occurs, neurotransmitters are sent to the brain, which in turn sends neurotransmitters to the injured area so that pain is induced to move from the stimuli. Even though we may see the injury the instant it occurs, it takes a moment to physically react.

Ésprit with SoZoKi

Another example that points away from the brain as our center of consciousness is what occurs while under general anesthesia. During a surgical procedure, the brain is kept asleep with gases, while powerful narcotics are given to block the pain our nervous system experiences. Experiential recall of events by patients who have undergone a surgical procedure has been cited again and again. Patients have described out of body experiences with their consciousness floating above their body, and were capable of giving a description of events that occurred during the surgery to which their anesthetized brain would not have had awareness.

Anatomical connections to this chakra are the male reproduction system, sex drive of both genders, and waste elimination. From the Root, energy flows to the testes, prostate, vagina, pelvis, tail bone, legs, and feet. The adrenals are the glands that drive this chakra because of their production of sex hormones rather than their location in the body. Rates of occurrence of prostate cancer for 2018 was estimated to be 164,700 [2], testicular cancer cases were estimated to be 9,310 [3] and 5,170 vaginal cancers diagnosis were predicted.[4] Peripheral vascular disease (PVD), along with total hip and knee replacements round out the myriad poor outcomes associated with blocked Root Chakras, when traumatic injury is not the known underlying

Ésprit with SoZoKi

cause.

The Root Chakra is identified as having masculine or *yang* properties and is identified as the vortex most closely connected to primal energy and the survival instinct. This connection is not limited to a flight-or-fight response that all life possesses for individual preservation, but it is also associated with reproduction and survival of the species. A stronger sex drive most often occurs at a higher level in the male of the species. Driven by hormones during the reproductive years, the design of this energy vortex ensures life continues on Earth. Yang tendencies include active energy, positivity, sunshine, daytime, aridness, upward-seeking, heavenly, fire, resoluteness, male, restless, productive, even numbers, domination, and heat/hot.

Foods that support an open and healthy Root Chakra are vegetables that grow within the earth such as potatoes, sweet potatoes, turnips, carrots, onions, garlic, ginger, and turmeric. Proteins like meat, eggs, nuts, and beans provide nourishment and enhanced energy flow to this chakra. Foods that are red in color also help to maintain health and open flow of the Root Chakra. These include tomatoes, strawberries, raspberries, cherries, pomegranates, and apples. Incorporate one or more of these foods into your diet daily to sustain the flow of Creation's energy.

Ésprit with SoZoKi

The sense associated with the Root is smell, the color is red, and the symbol is the square. Therefore, the use of shades of red, square symbology, a high-protein diet, and the fragrances of cinnamon, cedar, and myrrh, as well as the gemstone hematite, bloodstone, meditation on the planet Saturn, and the element of Earthy soil can all contribute to the cleansing and strengthening of the Root Chakra.

Cleansing allows the Root Chakra to open for maximum energy flow. An inexpensive way to accomplish this cleansing is to situate yourself by a cedar tree, sitting comfortably on a red blanket or towel with bare feet touching soil, and eating nuts while slowly drinking hot tea with cinnamon. Relax your mind and visualize the planet Saturn within its beautiful rings, while you slowly breathe in through your nose and out through your mouth.

Ésprit with SoZoKi

ROOT CHAKRA		
PRIME FUNCTION	POLARITY	DIVINE GOAL
Creation Energy enters Ethereal Body -- grounding, security, & survival. **Chakra of Inspired Thought**	**Positive**, pushing energy into the ethereal body via the Chakra System.	Maintain simplicity and **stability**
ANATOMY & SENSE	PROPERTY	HELP
Located **between thighs** and below trunk of body. **Organs Associated**: reproduction organs, sex drive all genders, waste elimination. Adrenal glands drive this chakra because of sex hormone production. **Sense is Smell**	**Yang tendencies** -- active energy, positivity, sunshine, daytime, and aridness, upward seeking, fire, resoluteness, domination, heat/hot.	**Foods:** vegetables grown in the earth, proteins, red colored foods **Scents:** cinnamon, cedar, myrrh **Gemstones:** Hematite, bloodstone **Metal:** Lead **Planet:** Saturn **Element:** Soil

3 - Sacral Chakra (Second)

The second energy vortex is known as the Sacral Chakra. It is located below the navel at the level of the bladder, and the polarity is negative, pulling energy into this vortex from the Root Chakra. As energy flows up from the Root, we experience intuition in the Sacral Chakra. When we are receptive to this intuition, it is conceptualized into an idea. When our Sacral Chakra is blocked or inhibited, we reject the insight, losing the opportunity to experience the inspired thought. Also with disfunction of the chakra, the internal organs associated with this chakra experience failure, dysfunction, and/or disease. When we reject intuited ideas and deny non-rational knowledge, we have ultimately rejected the natural flow of *SoZoKi*.

The primary function of the Sacral Chakra is the governance of emotions and relationships. Expression of the sexual and intimate aspects of our nature is attached to the energy of this vortex. When the chakra is open and energy is flowing freely, we experience intuitive understanding in our intimate relationships. We know that we are loved, have no need for constant reassurance; and we are inspired by this love. We understand that allowing freedom to individuate in a partnership results in a relationship unencumbered by fear of loss, and results in one of the highest expressions of a healthy Sacral Chakra. When this chakra is open and flowing, we are sensitive in our relationships. We easily give, and with equal ease, receive, responding to the needs and gifts of those who share our life.

This chakra is also associated with our creative life. When it is healthy we have a sense of "feeling alive" and creativity flows. When blocked we experience frustration in our creative process or even lose the ability to be creative. Creativity is not limited to art forms but figures also in everything from business ventures to lifestyle choices. When the Sacral Chakra is blocked, it can also manifest as illness, depleting or depressing our natural immune response.

A closed Sacral Chakra results in a loss of access to our intuitive process. In Western culture, intuition is pitted against a patriarchal, yang approach to life and the belief that a person experiences only that which can be objectively measured. Both men and women have often seen the feminine nature as hysterical, and intuitive thought as flights of

Ésprit with SoZoKi

fantasy lacking verifiable data to substantiate the experience. But denying our intuition in turn dampens our creative flow.

Subjective well-being has been studied by psychologists along with strategies to cope with moods. Thoughts of hopelessness enter our psyche and manifest as anxiety in Western cultures and clinical depression in Eastern cultures. Addressing cross-cultural rates of occurrence in Eastern and Western societies have uncovered a much higher incidence of anxiety and depressive experiences in the Western-based culture of the United States and Eastern in China. Psychologists attempt to understand why America reports to being a "happier" society than that China when it has a higher occurrence of reported anxiety and depressive episodes. For years it was believed that social norms in China caused under-reporting, but cross-cultural researchers are finding that speculation fails to hold truth, proposing that the difference in cultural views produces different responses to emotions. The world view of Western cultures is analytical while Eastern cultures hold a more holistic view. Eastern cultures believe opposites should coexist in interdependence with self-defined obligations and relations. Western thought processes isolate and objectify an idea of an independent self in their intra-personal interactions.[5]

Ésprit with SoZoKi

Anatomical associations with the Sacral Chakra include the spleen, kidneys and urinary tract system, ovaries, fallopian tubes, uterus, prostate, and testes. This energy vortex also works in conjunction with the third chakra, the Solar Plexus Chakra, to maintain normal blood sugar levels. The gonads, or reproductive glands, drive this chakra. The Divine principles of this energy vortex are sensitivity, sensual desire, reproduction, responding, giving, and receiving. When the flow of energy to and through this chakra is blocked or diminished you may experience difficulty in giving as well as receiving intimacy. A female may lose sexual desire when this chakra shuts down, limiting the opportunity to reproduce. Men with strong *yin* tendencies may have difficulty expressing emotions or experience loss of vitality or libido. This energy vortex has *yin* or feminine properties and is associated with such phenomena as passivity, negativity, darkness, mother earth or downward seeking, the night, northern slope, cloudiness or opacity, the Moon, water or moisture, slow approach, consuming, cold temperatures, odd numbers, and docile or soft aspects of things.
Under the influence of the Sacral Chakra, women often struggle to let go of emotions, negative communications, or actions, and they'll hold onto grudges of a perceived slight for a lifetime. A man, on the other hand, can have a physical fight with another man and then be seen sharing a drink and

Ésprit with SoZoKi

laughing at their actions shortly after the fight has ended.

The sense associated with the Sacral Chakra is taste and the color is orange. When you believe you need to support this energy vortex, consuming the following foods can help to stimulate and open the chakra. Orange being the color, the foods you should include in your diet are sweet potatoes, yams, mangos, oranges, peaches, apricots, orange peppers, and carrots. Foods rich in Omega-3 are also important for this chakra's health, so seek sources like salmon, sardines, oysters, olives, eggs, navy beans, chia seeds, soybeans, Brussel sprouts, and canola oil.

The Moon is the celestial body that helps to open a closed Sacral Chakra, and water is the associated element. The scents of dragon's blood, saffron, and rose will help increase energy flow through this vortex along with a diet that includes adequate fluid intake. The gemstone coral carnelian can be worn as jewelry or placed on an altar. To help heal this chakra, during a full moon, find a comfortable place in nature near a body of water; a creek, lake, ocean, or even a pool if none of the others are readily available to you. Wear jewelry or hold in your hand coral carnelian stones, have 8 to 16 ounces of your favorite liquid (it does not have to be water) with you and surround yourself with the scent you most enjoy. An hour spent in the environment you

Ésprit with SoZoKi

have created with a focus on the Sacral Chakra will help it to cleanse and open, allowing energy to flow freely.

Ésprit with SoZoKi

SACRAL CHAKRA

Prime Function	Polarity	Divine Goal
Governance of emotions and relationships. **Chakra of Intuition**	**Negative**, pulling energy up from the root on its ascent through the system.	**Sensitivity**, sensual desire, reproduction, giving, receiving & creativity

Anatomy & Sense	Property	Help
Located at the **level of the bladder**. **Organs Associated**: spleen, kidneys, urinary tract, ovaries, fallopian tubes, prostate & testes. **Sense is Taste**	**Yin tendencies** – passivity, negativity, darkness, mother earth or downward seeking, the night, northern slope, the Moon, water, moisture, cold temperatures.	**Foods**: orange colored and those rich in Omega-3 **Scents**: dragon's blood, saffron and rose **Gemstone**: Coral Carnelian **Planet**: Moon **Element**: Water **Metal**: Tin

Ésprit with SoZoKi

4 - *Solar Plexus Chakra (Third)*

The third energy vortex is identified as the Solar Plexus Chakra and is located just above the umbilicus, aka navel or belly button. The polarity of the solar plexus chakra is positive, pulling energy upward that is pushed from the negative polarity of the Sacral Chakra. The Solar Plexus Chakra then pushes energy upward into the Heart vortex. As inspiration and intuition flow through the first and second chakras, they arrive in the Solar Plexus where judgements or opinions are formed. When open, we accept the information provided by the Root and Sacral Chakra with positivity and grow the seed with integrated understanding. When this chakra is inhibited or closed we dismiss the thought processes that have developed as being insignificant or misguided, and we lose our intuition or gut feeling.

The prime function of the Solar Plexus Chakra is coordinating energy, vitality, and willpower with our desires and is considered our body's battery. When energy flows freely through this chakra, we have a sense of purpose, our state of mind is energized, and we experience our own autonomy. The Divine principle of this chakra is inner strength. With self-control we are efficient, pay attention to details and achieve the best results from the effort we apply. We need this vortex to function because when it does not, we fall victim to selfishness. When it is obstructed we lack personal authority, and we seek power through the control of others rather than through self-control. Characteristic behaviors from aloofness to intimidation emerge to seek and draw energy from those with whom we interact. We fall victim to anger, fail at goals and have a sense of purposeless existence.

When energy flow dwindles or is blocked, organs and systems associated with this chakra experience states of disease, dysfunction, or failure. Organ connections to the Solar Plexus Chakra include the stomach, gallbladder, liver and small intestine, and in particular, the pancreas. According to the National Institutes of Health (NIH), there are approximately 20 million people in this country with gallstones, 300,000 cholecystectomies (surgical removal of the gall bladder) are performed annually, and 15% of the population have asymptomatic gallstones.[6] All of these disorders are influenced by the health of the Solar Plexus Chakra.

Through 25 years as an operating room nurse and having interviewed tens of thousands of patients, I have always been intrigued by the number of people in the United States who have reported that they suffer from gastroesophageal reflux disease (GERD). In a *Digestive Diseases and Science* research article published on NCBI in 2014, the authors noted a steady rise in the rate of occurrence in industrialized countries around the globe. Annually there more than 9 million visits to primary care doctors with complaints of GERD. The related utilization of sick day absences has posed a financial burden on both patient and their employer. GERD has also imposed a financial burden on health care systems.[7]

How many medications have been developed to stop acid in the stomach from rising up into the esophagus with a burning sensation often mimicking a heart attack? Television commercials are relentless in identifying the cause as a physical ailment to be treated with medication, but not exploring the connections to our spiritual state of health. GERD is the symptom, but is it a consequence of anatomical or ethereal dis-ease? We need to look for both pathologies in order to find lasting relief.

Judgement is the ability to make a decision, or form an opinion objectively, authoritatively, and wisely. In current western cultures, judgements are frequently formed after, and on the basis of, subjective opinions. When we witness what we believe to be a bad action, we identify it as such. When we identify the person rather than their behavior as bad, we have applied judgement upon the person. They have been judged as a bad person, rather than they performed a bad action.

We in America live in a predominantly Christian-Judeo religious culture that teaches to "judge not lest you be judged" or "he who is without sin cast the first stone" yet how many times a day do people judge one another? Judgements are formed after, and on the basis of, opinions. To put it another way, judgements are applied opinions, and having judged, we expect gratitude for our wisdom!

The Solar Plexus Chakra is identified as androgynous in nature and ideally exists in a state of unified duality. Connected to both yin and yang, feminine and masculine, it represents the surrender of each to the other. This chakra is dominated by neither property but exists as the same energy

Ésprit with SoZoKi

vortex in females and males, and it is subject to a melting-pot of emotions, both positive and negative.

The color yellow is associated with the Solar Plexus and sight is the sense. Dietary considerations to ensure the health of this chakra include lentils, beans, chickpeas, bananas, lemons, and pineapple. Chamomile consumed as tea and the spices ginger, cinnamon, turmeric, and cumin in recipes support the energy flow through the Solar Plexus. Scents of ginger, blueberry, and cedar are also identified with this chakra. These scents, along with the gemstone amber citrine and a diet sufficient in grains, help cleanse this chakra.

Mars is the planet associated with this energy vortex and fire is the element. Heat supports and increases energy flow to the Solar Plexus Chakra. A walk in the sunshine, time spent in front of a fireplace, or even an infrared sauna can help open this chakra. Yoga poses, including planking and other poses that engage the body's core, help to stimulate the Solar Plexus, increasing the flow of energy out of the vortex to the entire body. A yellow yoga mat, the scent of cedar burning in your fireplace, and the presence of amber citrine will help to cleanse this chakra for maximum performance.

SOLAR PLEXUS CHAKRA

Prime Function	Polarity	Divine Goal
Judgement and Opinion **Chakra of vitality, willpower & coordinator of energy – The Body's Battery**	**Positive**, pulls energy from Sacral Chakra.	**Inner Strength**, sense of purpose, mind is energized
Anatomy & Sense	Property	Help
Located **above the navel** (bellybutton) **Organs Associated:** stomach, gallbladder, liver and small intestine, and in particular, the pancreas **Sense is Sight**	**Androgynous** -- ideally exists in a state of unified duality. Subject to a melting pot of emotions, both positive and negative.	**Foods**: lentils, beans, chickpeas, bananas, lemons, and pineapple; ginger, cumin, cinnamon, and turmeric. **Scents**: of ginger, blueberry, and cedar **Gemstone**: amber citrine **Planet**: Mars **Element**: Fire **Metal**: Iron

5 - Heart Chakra (Fourth)

The fourth energy vortex resides in the center of the chest and is known as the Heart Chakra. Polarity for this chakra is negative, pulling energy from the Solar Plexus and pushing energy to the Throat vortex. As energy flows into this chakra from the Solar Plexus, the judgment or opinion on the intuition and inspiration is given a second chance, as reconsideration emerges and opportunity for change occurs. When the flow of energy through this vortex is diminished or blocked, we miss the opportunity to replace negative with positive thoughts or intentions.

The prime function of the Heart Chakra is balanced love and connection. As the center of love for self, others, nature, and the Divine, it provides emotional equilibrium. It is also where ego resides and hope springs eternal. When this energy vortex is blocked or diminished, we lose our ability to be flexible, holding only to rigid beliefs and behaviors. Our coping abilities decline. Feelings of trust and the impulse to share go missing, inhibiting our ability to love or be loved, and organs and body systems may exhibit disease or even failure.

The Divine principles or goals of this chakra include forgiveness, sharing, respect, and openness to one another and to circumstance. So when open, energy flows to and through this chakra, and we experience compassion for ourselves and others, and are lifted by a positive attitude. Hope resides in the forefront of our thought processes.

Anatomical connections and systems impacted by the Heart Chakra include cardiac function (heart, circulation, blood pressure), lungs, lymphatic and immune systems, as well as allergies. The gland that governs this chakra is the thymus, an organ which is closely aligned with the immune system in its responsibility for the production of the white blood cells that defend our bodies against infection.

According to the Centers for Disease Control and Prevention (CDC), approximately 610,000 people in the United States die annually from heart disease; it's the cause of one in every four deaths. Coronary artery disease alone kills over 370,000. More than 735,000 people experience a heart attack annually.[8]

Ésprit with SoZoKi

Each year the NIH, in conjunction with the American Heart Association (AHA), the CDC and other government agencies, produces a single document with the most current statistics concerning heart disease and stroke, and factors that contribute to their outcomes. According to research, the core behaviors impacting the health of the cardiovascular system include smoking, diet, physical activity, and weight. These factors directly impact the systemic functions of blood pressure regulation, glucose control, and cholesterol levels. [9] But missing from the government data, as might be expected from Western medicine authorities, is any mention of the potential role blocked energy may play in the development or outcomes of these diseases.

As reported by the American Lung Association (ALA) in 2015, the estimated prevalence for the lung illnesses identified as chronic obstructive pulmonary disease (COPD) in the America, which include emphysema and bronchitis, was over 11 million cases, with many remaining undiagnosed. [10] The estimated prevalence of asthma, as reported by the U.S. Environmental Protection Agency (EPA) in their 2018 report based on 2015-16 statistics, was 24.6 million people, of whom 6.1 million are children. [11]

Ésprit with SoZoKi

In the article *Allergy Statistics and Facts*, published on December 1, 2017 by webmd.com, 30% of adults and 40% of children in the United States have allergies to a wide variety of substances. At least 40 million Americans experience allergic symptoms on a regular basis.[12] According to the American Autoimmune Related Diseases Association, 20% of our population, or one in five Americans suffer from an autoimmune disease.[13] Missing from this Western medical statistical data, and from the research that supports it, is the potential role that blocked energy flow plays in body system dysfunction.

The Heart Chakra possesses transformative *yin* properties. Dark moist places yielding to the Creation of new life correspond to the ability to reconsider opinions and judgments made in the Solar Plexus, giving birth metaphorically to new opinions by means of processing and removing dysfunctional critical judgments. The Heart Chakra can, however, when unhealthy, nurture grudges and unreleased judgmental thinking.

Green is the color of the Heart Chakra and the sense associated with it is touch. Diets to support the health of this chakra are filled with greens, both vegetables and fruits. Herbs and green algae supplements are valuable as well. Spinach, kale,

Ésprit with SoZoKi

zucchini, Brussels sprouts, green beans, Asian greens, peas, broccoli, and asparagus serve to open and maintain this energy vortex. Helpful fruits include limes, kiwi, avocado, green grapes, apples, and cucumbers. You can also consume herbs such as mint, parsley, coriander, oregano, tarragon, thyme, sage, and basil, as well as superfoods like wheatgrass, spirulina, barley grass and green tea to ensure the health of the Heart Chakra.

The planet Venus rules our Heart Chakra and the associated element is air. Scents of heliotrope, chamomile, and rose will enhance energy flow through this vortex as will the gemstones green tourmaline and kunzite, worn as jewelry or resting on a surface in your environment in their natural state. If you live outside of a metropolitan area it can be easy to take an evening stroll, breathing in the fresh air with awareness and intention. If living in an urban area, I would recommend a daytrip to the countryside for a hike or bike ride, to breath in the cleansing freshness of our natural world.

If Venus is in its evening star phase and you can stay long enough after sunset, look for the bright planet and spend some time meditating on its unbridled magnificence. (Halfway through its 19-month cycle Venus will become retrograde and disappear from the night sky for 40 days, returning

Ésprit with SoZoKi

as the morning star, visible just before sunrise.) Surround yourself with the scent you most enjoy, wear or hold the gemstone you have chosen, and drink a glass of green tea to keep yourself hydrated with a fluid that heals or enhances your Heart Chakra.

Ésprit with SoZoKi

HEART CHAKRA

Prime Function	Polarity	Divine Goal
Balanced love and connection. **Chakra of LOVE**	**Negative**, pulling energy up from the Solar Plexus and pushing to Throat Chakra.	**Forgiveness**, sharing, respect, and openness to one another and to circumstance.
Anatomy & Sense	**Property**	**Help**
Located in the **center of the chest**. **Organs Associated**: cardiac function (heart, circulation, blood pressure), lungs, lymphatic and immune systems, as well as allergies **Sense is Touch**	**Yin tendencies** – passivity, negativity, darkness, mother earth or downward seeking, the night, northern slope, the Moon, water, moisture, cold temperatures.	**Foods**: greens, both vegetables and fruits. **Scents**: heliotrope, chamomile, and rose **Gemstone**: Green tourmaline and Kunzite **Planet**: Venus **Element**: Air **Metal**: Copper

6 - Throat Chakra (Fifth)

The fifth energy vortex is known as the Throat Chakra and is located mid-neck. The polarity of this chakra is positive, pulling energy from the negative polar aspect of the Heart and pushing into the negative polarity of the Third Eye Chakra. As energy has flowed through the preceding chakras, inspiration and intuition that has been integrated into the first three vortices, with the opportunity to be transformed in the fourth or Heart Chakra, it reaches the throat and gives rise to what we communicate to the world.

When the chakra system is open, and the Heart Chakra is fully functional, we have the capacity to produce positive communication. When closed or dysfunctional our vocalizations become negative, seeking to denounce or denigrate rather than lift or elevate those with whom we interact. While Creation Energy always flows from a source that is positive in charge, impaired lower chakras can twist the intent. Evil can be described as bad decisions made by our conscious, human mind, and we must acknowledge and accept responsibility for our own behavior rather than fall prey to the tendency to blame an external evil which "forced" poor decision-making upon us, denying our freewill (i.e., "The devil made me do it").

The Throat Chakra's prime functions are communication and healing. The Divine Goal is purpose in life. Our creative process is also aligned here, and it is the vortex that provides the ability to see others as whole individuals and acknowledge the One Will of the Creator. The energy of language is filled with powerful words which have the ability to heal and lift higher, but in a negative framework can humiliate, harm, hinder, or humble. As we interact with others, it is through this chakra that we can stimulate goodness, convey appreciation and respect, and offer comfort, but it can also be the means to disparage and denigrate. Speech can be used to divide-and-conquer or fracture unity through criticism, defamation, and divisiveness.

Anatomical connections associated with the Throat Chakra include throat, neck, ears, sinus, parathyroid and the upper respiratory system. The gland that governs it is the thyroid. In the United States, there are around 100,000 new cases of parathyroid disease diagnosed annually. [14] The American Thyroid Associated (ATA) reports more than 12% of our population will develop thyroid disease during their lifetimes. An estimated 20 million Americans have already been diagnosed with some kind of thyroid disease. [15] Although it is a very small organ, the thyroid produces a stimulating hormone (TSH) which influences every cell in our body and is ultimately responsible for regulating metabolism (the chemical processes within an organism that maintain life). Statista's statistics portal has reported expected revenue from the sales of cold and cough medicines in the United States to be as high as $8,977 billion in 2018 and rising rapidly. [16] According to the CDC, 26.9 million Americans are diagnosed with a sinus infection annually. [17] While ear infections do occur within adult populations, they are predominately found in young children. Often these infections of the ear canals in children will correct with age, however, left untreated these infections can lead to hearing loss or deafness in severe cases.

The Throat Chakra possesses masculine or *yang* tendencies and when energy is flowing freely to and through this vortex, active energy, positivity, upward-seeking, heavenly, and productive aspects arise. Communication is positive, engaging without judgment, and conciliatory or collaborative in nature. When energy is blocked or diminished we can see a tendency towards dominance and unwavering resoluteness in the communication style.

Hearing, you might think ironically, is the sense associated with the Throat Chakra, but communication comprises both speaking and listening. While it is important to vocalize our thoughts, it is equally important to be an active listener. When we insist on dominating a conversation, and deny another's chance to be heard, we are experiencing a decrease or block in energy flow through this vortex.

Diets to support the health of this chakra include adequate amounts of fluid intake to ensure your throat is lubricated. Sore or scratchy throats inhibit our natural speech-patterns, so make sure you are not mistaking a chakra issue with a simple lack of fluid intake. The color blue is associated with the Throat Chakra, and while there is a limited number of natural blue foods available for consumption, blueberries, blue corn, blue potatoes and edible flowers such as borage and blue orchids offer support to this chakra. Tree fruits that naturally fall

Ésprit with SoZoKi

when ripe such as peaches, plums, mangos, and avocados are a great source of hydration for additional food support. Blueberry smoothies, yogurt, pies and cobblers, and salads with edible flowers are appetizing ways to include a boost to your diet to benefit this energy vortex.

Mercury is the planet associated with the Throat Chakra, and ether is the element. In this context ether refers to the upper regions of space, clear skies or heaven, rather than a chemical or physical property. The scents of eucalyptus, frankincense, and sandalwood will enhance the flow of energy to and through this vortex, and turquoise and azurite gemstones are used to bring focused energy to it.

When you want to work on the energy flowing to and through the Throat Chakra, try the following or develop your own scenario using the information provided above. Fashion your environment using the color blue, wear or hold your chosen gemstone, incorporate your favorite associated scent, and if possible, drink Thai Butterfly Pea Tea made with organic dried blue flowers before you start your mediation. If you cannot find this tea, a bowl of blueberries is a great source of naturally occurring antioxidants that will help in reversing inflammatory responses in your physical body. Observing the element of ether's association with

Ésprit with SoZoKi

this chakra, use the guided meditation provided in the final chapter of this book. Rather than sending your ethereal body deep into Earth's energy, I suggest a mild grounding to Earth's energy, then reaching the energy of all of Creation, *SoZoKi*.

Ésprit with SoZoKi

THROAT CHAKRA

Prime Function	Polarity	Divine Goal
Communication and healing. **Chakra of the One Will of the Creator**	**Positive**, pulls energy from the Heart Chakra.	**Purpose in life,** creativity and Divine Love.

Anatomy & Sense	Property	Help
Located **mid-neck**. **Organs Associated**: throat, neck, ears, sinus, parathyroid and the upper respiratory system. The gland that governs it is the thyroid. **Sense is Hearing**	**Yang tendencies** – active energy, positivity, sunshine, daytime, and aridness, upward seeking, fire, resoluteness, domination, heat/hot.	**Foods**: blueberries, blue corn. Tree fruits such as peaches, plums, mangos, and avocados. **Scents**: eucalyptus, frankincense, and sandalwood **Gemstone**: turquoise and azurite **Planet**: Mercury **Element**: Ether **Metal**: Mercury

7 - Third Eye Chakra (Sixth)

The sixth energy vortex is known as the Third Eye, and it is located above the eyebrows in the middle of the forehead and thought to be connected to the brain. The polarity of the Third Eye Chakra is negative, pulling energy from the positive aspect of the Throat Chakra and pushing energy to the Crown. As energy flows into this chakra from the throat, inspiration, intuition, judgement, re-evaluation and communication have all taken place. It is in this chakra that we come to an understanding of our place in Creation. When we acknowledge the pattern and flow of energy that occurred in the first five chakras, we find ourselves able to accept that we are united with all that exists, neither above, below, nor separate in any way from all else. This chakra is considered to be the seat of our celestial body.

It is within the Third Eye that imagination emerges and where we open our spirit fully to *SoZoKi*.

Ésprit with SoZoKi

When energy is blocked or diminished we may find it difficult to learn new skills. Our memory and pattern recognition, which are the basis of our ability to classify data and experience, may be impaired.

The prime function of the Third Eye is integration and understanding. It is through this vortex that we are able to see beyond the five physiologic senses of our anatomical body. The Third Eye Chakra is considered the center of clairvoyance, and it is here that we have our sixth sense, our psychic ability, the sense residing within our celestial rather than physical body. The Divine principle of this chakra is the use of imagination and clairvoyance to see our spirit as it relates to all Creation.

Anatomical connections to this energy vortex include the brow, eyes, hypothalamus, and autonomic nervous system (which regulates unconscious bodily functions such as circulation of the blood, respiration, and digestion; aka., homeostasis). The gland that governs this chakra is the pituitary, which is considered the master gland of the entire endocrine system due to the immense variety and volume of hormones it releases into the bloodstream. Hormones responsible for maintaining optimal states of hydration and blood pressure, producing breast milk, stimulating

Ésprit with *SoZoKi*

growth, and developing eggs in females and sperm in males, among other essential functions, originate in or are stimulated by the pituitary gland.

In 2014, the NIH's National Eye Institute estimated the annual economic burden of vision loss, disorders, or disease to be a whopping $139 million. There are 1.3 million Americans diagnosed as legally blind (20/200 vision), and this number is predicted to reach 2.2 million by 2030. Another 2.9 million Americans have been diagnosed with low vision, and that figure is expected to rise to 5 million by 2030. Major eye diseases afflicting Americans include age-related macular degeneration (2.1 million), glaucoma (2.7 million), diabetic retinopathy (7.7 million), and cataracts (24 million). Similar increases are predicted for the occurrence of refractive errors, standing in 2014 at 34.1 million for nearsightedness and 14.1 million for farsightedness. [18.]

The Graham Headache Center in Boston, along with Brigham and Women's Hospital and Harvard Medical School, gathered data from the National Health Interview Survey completed in 2012 and reported by the National Institutes of Health in 2015. At that time, 14.2% of American adults over 18 years of age reported migraine or severe headaches during a 3-month period. (Females experienced migraine headaches at a rate of 19.1% and males 9% [19]

The hypothalamus, located mid-brain and between the ears, also releases hormones that regulate body temperature, mood, and hunger. Some genetic disorders and birth defects have been traced to dysfunction of this gland. Perimenopausal vasomotor symptoms, more commonly known as hot flashes, occurring in 75-80% of American women, is now believed to be caused by a diminished function of the hypothalamus due to decreased estrogen production. [20]

As is the Solar Plexus, the Third Eye Chakra is identified as having an androgynous property, the state of unified duality. Connected to both *yin* and *yang*, it embodies the surrender of each to the other. Not dominated by either alone, the Third Eye energy vortex is the same in females and males and is the seat of a melting-pot of emotions, both positive and negative.

Indigo is the color of the Third Eye Chakra, the color of perceptiveness and service to humanity, conveying integrity and dignity. Clairvoyance, or the ability to see beyond the physical, is the sense associated with this energy vortex, and it is strongly associated with the intuitive abilities in a healthy, high-functioning Sacral Chakra. We intuit

Ésprit with SoZoKi

in the Sacral and then see in totality with the Third Eye when energy is freely flowing to and through the chakras.

Including purple or dark blue fruits and vegetables in your diet will assist in opening this chakra and keep energy flowing. Blackberries, blueberries, black currants, purple grapes, prunes, and plums are fruits that can boost energy flow to this chakra as well as provide powerful antioxidants in their naturally occurring state. Vegetables to consume include purple cabbage, potatoes, peppers, and asparagus. Along with these fruits and vegetables, a diet rich in Omega-3s is important to stave off dementia and depression, so include nuts, avocados, salmon, flaxseed and olives. Dark chocolate stimulates the release of serotonin, the "feel-good" hormone, and promotes mental clarity. A diet filled with these recommended foods will nourish and develop our sixth sense housed in the Third Eye.

Jupiter is the planet aligned with this chakra and the element is light. Scents of lavender, star anise, and galangal (blue Thai ginger) will all increase energy flow to and within your Third Eye. The gemstones lapis and amethyst, and the metal silver, are associated with this chakra. As with the other vortexes, surrounding yourself with the images, scents, and gemstones associated with the Third Eye will maintain or serve to restore health.

Along with diet, a variety of yoga poses will increase energy flow to this chakra. Poses that push energy upward include Tree, Eagle, Child, Warrior Three, and Downward Facing Dog. Surround yourself with your chosen scent, unroll your indigo color yoga mat, and center your meditative focus on the Third Eye as you move through these and other yoga poses. If you choose to meditate on Jupiter, you will find it is usually the third brightest object in the night sky (after Venus and the Moon) and is best seen in the southeastern night sky when it reaches opposition with the Sun every 13 months.

Ésprit with SoZoKi

THIRD EYE CHAKRA

Prime Function	Polarity	Divine Goal
Integration and understanding. **Chakra is center of celestial body.**	**Negative**, pulls energy from the Throat Chakra.	**Imagination & Clairvoyance** to see our spirit as it relates to all Creation.

Anatomy & Sense	Property	Help
Located above the eyebrows in the middle of the forehead. **Organs Associated**: brow, eyes, hypothalamus, and autonomic nervous system (which regulates unconscious bodily functions such as circulation of the blood, respiration, and digestion). **Sense is Psychic Ability**	**Androgynous** -- ideally exists in a state of unified duality. Subject to a melting pot of emotions, both positive and negative, is the same in females and males.	**Foods**: Blackberries, blueberries, black currants, purple grapes, prunes, and plums. Purple cabbage, potatoes, peppers, and asparagus. **Scents:** lavender, star anise, and galangal **Gemstone**: lapis, amethyst **Metal:** Silver **Planet**: Jupiter **Element:** Light

Ésprit with SoZoKi

Ésprit with SoZoKi

8 - Crown Chakra (Seventh)

The seventh energy vortex, which completes the major chakra system, is known as the Crown, the center of enlightenment. The polarity of the Crown is positive, pushing energy out to *SoZoKi*, as completion connects us to the Divine before pushing *SoZoKi* back into the Root Chakra as its positive polarity pulls and continues the energy circuit. This Chakra has an exogenous property, meaning it is derived from an external source outside of an organism and is the second vortex where the lines of meridian cross 21 times outside of our physical body. Just as the Root is swirling below what is often identified at the trunk of our body, the Crown is swirling above the top of our head. While the Root is masculine in nature, providing positive *SoZoKi* that fires up our energy system when open and functioning, it is the exogeneity of the Crown that sustains both our physical and ethereal bodies.

Ésprit with SoZoKi

While the Third Eye focuses on our place in Creation, it is the Crown that attaches us to *SoZoKi* and maintains the energy flow when the chakras are open and functioning freely. As energy exits the Crown, it circles back to the Root in a continuous cycle of spirit and sense.

Our acceptance of *something greater than our self* is essential, even though we may not understand or even be aware of this energy system. It is with a well-developed and high functioning Crown Chakra that our spirit surpasses human consciousness, and the stories we have told ourselves -- the explanations of how life works -- fade away to self-actualization. Does this mean we will no longer experience pain, suffering, or loneliness? No, it does not. What it does mean is the self-centered idea of being, the thought we only need to be accountable for those in our family, tribe or religious communities, fades and we come to understanding that while our spirit may be housed in an individual body and mind, it is a part of something far larger and greater than all that we know and have yet to know exists.

The prime function of the Crown energy vortex is enlightenment and transcendence. Spiritual understanding transforms into spirit consciousness. The Divine principle is divinity in the company of higher values and wisdom. Inspiration, higher reason, and awareness are the goals associated with the Divine's *SoZoKi*.

Anatomical connections include the central nervous system, head, cerebral cortex, upper spine, and hair. The gland that governs this energy vortex is the pineal which is a pea-sized structure located in the middle of the brain. The function is to release hormones that regulate sleep patterns or what is identified as circadian rhythm. When we look at life, it is filled with rhythms -- tides, moon, season, sleep, and reproduction cycles are but a few that readily come to mind.

While the natural world adheres to these cycles, day in and day out, month in and month out, year in and year out, we humans seem intent on finding ways to live in conflict with Nature. Most of us need 7 to 8 hours of sleep every 24 hours, and on a regular schedule. Some people work at night and sleep during the day, which for most produces considerable strain. A great many people are sleep-deprived due to eating or drinking the wrong things close to bedtime, or watching television programs that keep our brain active when it should be quiet. These activities inhibit the benefit of the pineal hormone, melatonin, to induce the quietude that allows us to naturally fall easily into sleep each

Ésprit with SoZoKi

night.

Another common challenge to the natural system is the use of a variety of birth control measures to stop or change reproductive cycles. More dramatic, as an operating room nurse I have witnessed, again and again, families keeping loved ones alive past their natural life cycle, often putting them through horrific medical procedures, because they love them so much (if not so well) that they can't let them go naturally back to the Divine. This is not to say we should not do what we can to remain in this life, to fulfill the intention of our spirit. As I participated in surgical procedures, not just in one hospital in one town, but in 23 hospitals in 23 cities in 11 states across the country, one theme became apparent to me. When it is time for our spirit to leave this life, it is time, and when it is not, it is not. No matter the intervention or lack thereof, it is the Spirit attached to the Divine that ends the life of the physical body.

Central nervous system disorders and disease include, but are not limited to, Alzheimer's, Bell's and cerebral palsy, epilepsy, motor neuron disease, multiple sclerosis, neurofibromatosis, and Parkinson's Disease. The Alzheimer's Association has reported that in 2018 an estimated 5.7 million Americans are living with this disease. [21] The

Ésprit with SoZoKi

NIH's National Institute of Neurological Disorders and Stroke reported an estimated 40,000 people experience Bell's palsy and the CDC has reported an estimated 795,000 strokes occur annually in this country. [22, 23] The Parkinson's Foundation reported by 2020 nearly 1 million in the United States will be living with the disease with approximately 60,000 new cases diagnosed each year. Internationally more than 10 million have been diagnosed and are living with it. [24]

The color associated with the Crown Chakra is a purplish white we identify as violet (light purple). Often identified with power, royalty, and wealth in the secular world, it is also the color that corresponds with wisdom, sensitivity, nurturing, imagination, creativity, and sacredness in spiritual realms. The sense associated with this energy vortex is thought: the capacity to think, contemplate, consider, and reason.

There are no specific foods associated with improving or maintaining energy flow to and through the Crown Chakra as it is housed in the ethereal or spiritual realm. That being said, it is important to ensure you are consuming a healthy, well-balanced diet filled with the food sources mentioned for each of the first through sixth energy vortices. Every body is different in how it metabolizes or uses the food we eat. Some do well with a high-protein low-carbohydrate diet, others are vegetarian or vegan, while some follow a paleo diet. (Short for paleolithic, it's typically a diet of meat, fruit, vegetables, and nuts as would have been consumed in that era.)

Just as it is important for the health of the body to find balance through nutrition and exercise, the ethereal and physical bodies need nutrition and exercise, although they are very different. Food and physical exertion for the body translates to meditation, mindfulness, prayer, energy practices, and held yoga posing. But also included are acts of kindness, open-mindedness, gratitude, service, a willingness to listen and to share experiences for understanding something that is not physically seen but actualized through our actions and interactions.

We are all role models. People are almost always watching and either consciously or subconsciously determining if they agree or disagree with another's words or actions. This does not mean that people always choose good over bad behavior. As you look around and see people of all backgrounds, cultures, and ages, it is good to keep in mind that they are souls or spirits on their own evolutionary path. Whether they are young or old souls, each has something to teach and learn while walking this life's path.

The planet associated with the Crown Chakra is Uranus, the seventh planet from the sun. While it is difficult to view with the naked eye, it can be seen by those with exceptional eyesight under the right conditions, but you may want to use binoculars to ensure you see it. Considered the largest ice giant, it was named after the Greek god of the sky, Ouranos. Pronounced Oo-RAH-nos, it is the only non-Roman-named planet. While spending time with this planet, although it may be difficult, it is the difficulty that brings intention and focus, as we commune with the Divine to enhance our Crown Chakra and connection to *SoZoKi*.

The element associated with the Crown is the same as the sense, that being thought. Scents for this energy vortex include jasmine, lotus, and peony. Gemstones to work with to increase energy flow to and through the Crown Chakra are diamonds, tourmaline, and clear quartz. The metal for this chakra is gold.

To clear blocks and open this chakra you will need to begin with fasting, but only if this does not interfere with the health of the body. Those with diagnosed medical conditions like hypoglycemia and diabetes should always work with their

Ésprit with SoZoKi

advanced care practitioners before attempting to fast. If it is safe for you to proceed, find a quiet environment where you will not be distracted, surround yourself with a chosen scent, and set aside time to hold yoga poses and/or meditate. Holding poses allows the mind to focus and fall naturally into a meditative state. A rolling breath meditation (see Chapter 10 for a detailed description) with all exterior stimuli removed is also another effective approach to focus on your attachment to the Divine's *SoZoKi*.

Ésprit with SoZoKi

CROWN CHAKRA		
PRIME FUNCTION	POLARITY	DIVINE GOAL
Center of enlightenment **Chakra of enlightenment and transcendence**	**Positive**, pulls energy from the Third Eye.	**Divinity** in the company of higher values and wisdom.
ANATOMY & SENSE	PROPERTY	HELP
Located above the top of our head. **Organs Associated**: central nervous system, head, cerebral cortex, upper spine, and hair. **Sense is Thought**	**Exogenous** sustaining physical & ethereal bodies	**Foods**: none associated – maintain healthy diet. Food & physical exertion for the body translates to meditation, mindfulness, prayer, energy practices, and held yoga poses. **Scents**: jasmine, lotus, and peony **Gemstone**: diamonds, tourmaline, and clear quartz **Planet**: Uranus **Element**: Thought **Metal**: Gold

Ésprit with SoZoKi

9 - SoZoKi Self-Practice

Starting & Ending Each Day

For many people, the practice of a morning ritual is to sleep as long as possible before rising to a rush of activity as they ready themselves for work, appointments, or life's everyday tasks. Parents are in demand to manage the routines that send children off to school and pets that need to go outside. All of these needs focus thought on what has to be accomplished. A healthier alternative is to go to sleep earlier and wake up unrushed so that you can take time to purposefully greet the day with gratitude and wonder before then setting your course for action on your day.

This is all easy for me to say because I do my best to ensure I do not have to get up and rush to meet my day. I prefer to take my time, going to bed early if needed, so that when I awake I can pet my dogs,

Ésprit with SoZoKi

drink my coffee, and then workout. I don't rush through a shower, throw on clothes and run out the door to jump in my car and drive off to work. Unrushed, I like to listen to some music or check the news of the day.

Sometimes I turn on an entertaining television show but then again I might just sit quietly to listen to a bird sing its song. While I have some sort of routine, I try not to be rigid with it, mixing it up a bit so that I enjoy the start of each day as something new or different. Routines are a way to get things accomplished but they can also make life mundane, following the same steps each morning, day in and day out. They can also dull your imagination, and at the same time (existing with something else, often in a lessor way) limit your spiritual growth.

If you are the sort of person who wakes with dread and immediately begins to think about the day ahead from a negative point of view, give yourself a way to turn that behavior around. It may be that you write a positive statement on a post-it note that is stuck to your bathroom mirror. If you are a sleepy head, you might choose to play music that is upbeat and makes you want to continue listening instead of falling back to sleep. Most importantly, get enough sleep!

Ésprit with SoZoKi

Getting enough sleep is easier said than done if you can't easily fall asleep. The good news is there is a variety of ways to help the process. First, stop stimulating yourself a couple of hours before you head to bed. No news on the TV or talk radio, no action movies or horror shows, and that goes for reading as well. Some people readily fall asleep after reading one page; that would be me. But for others, once they start reading they are lost for hours in the book and before they know it they have left themselves just a few hours to sleep before they start the next day. A tired person is not functioning on all of their cylinders and thus usually is an unhappy person. And unhappy people unwittingly invite negative encounters.

I typically do not have trouble falling to sleep, but on those occasions when my mind won't stop, I turn to new age music and connecting *SoZoKi*. I choose new age, you may choose another genre, the important aspect here is to ensure it is only an instrumental piece you choose. Words are powerful and will distract you from your mission - to fall into sleep. For other intentions in purposely attaching to *SoZoKi*, the sequence begins with the Root rather than Crown, to bring in and then move energy through your ethereal body. I describe in the next chapter the sequence of hand positions

Ésprit with SoZoKi

based on your intention for increasing *SoZoKi*, e.g., resolve sleeplessness, promote healing of a physical injury, meditation for the entire energy body and specific chakra focus. Other opportunities to calm your mind include meditation, yoga, the scent of lavender, and chamomile tea. The idea is to not overstimulate your mind to allow thinking to stop so that sleep finds its way to you. How you end your day impacts how you begin the next. This poem was inspired as I awoke in March of 2001.

<u>Fresh New Beginnings</u>

Can you feel the earth move, sense a low vibration?
Wheels on a distant road rushing to a new location?
When you look up at the clouds, what is it you see?
White on a blue canvas -- images appear to me.

What do you hear when a bird sings his song?
He will carry a melody if I listen well and long.
And when you first awake, what is it you feel?
Fresh, as-yet unburdened? Can that peace be real?

Ésprit with SoZoKi

A fresh new beginning is found in each sunrise,
Yesterday has passed. Will you allow this day to surprise?
Look at yourself, the one you know, the 'you' down deep inside
Hold that image in your mind, as each moment in life glides

To weave a unique story, the one that is called your life
When you advocate for love, your endeavor serves to replace strife
With love that finds its way to heart and then into your mind.
You will find your spirit at play, releasing what life has confined.

So, find your peace within each day, it's something we all possess!
Believe in purpose in your life, and try not to always test
Your faith in the Creator, who dwells in each of us
For life will quicken before our eyes as the body returns to dust.

03.15.01 / 07.17.19 / 11.15.2020

Ésprit with SoZoKi

Creating Your Space

Some may call it creating their altar, you may call it designing your intentional thought and behavior place. It does not matter what you call the space you create, it is only important you do it. Consider how and when you will use your space, will anyone participate with you? When desiring to change your perspective from half-empty to half-full; when deciding to raise your behaviors from health-ending to strength-building, the time you spend planning a sustainable choice is essential to successful outcomes.

Planning, practice, and time. Yes, it takes time to turn an extended period of negative anything into a consistent positive life practice. Think about how long you may have been approaching life with a half empty glass. Was it during your childhood, adolescence, young adulthood, as an older adult? The longer you've been displaying negative behaviors, the more effort you need to put into planning. Mostly, it is extremely important that you are honest with yourself! You and only you know every little weakness you possess, and you need to own them all, each and every one them.

Ensure you can freely speak to each item in the space. You must consider everything from the floor up. Include electricity and light control, ventilation,

Ésprit with SoZoKi

audio/visual capability, multiple seating opportunities (traditional chair or comfortable beanbag), space for a yoga mat to pose, the type of hydration you will need based on your practice session intention (water, tea, electrolytes), how you will provide aromatherapy (candles, incense, vaporizer, atomizer), and any religious talisman important to your spiritual belief. You may choose to light a candle of a chakra color, burn incense to cleanse an energy center, listen to an inspiring piece of music or set up to follow yoga posing, in a very cold, hot, or breezy atmosphere. Work with what you have in your life, don't use your current location as a barrier to your success. In my mother's words, "Don't be your own worst enemy, Nancy... Can't Never Could!"

As you return to this sacred space you have created for yourself, as you practice meditation, as you practice self-healing or healing another, energy will increase and your ability to engage energy to heal expands. Use of the Reiki symbols, (*cho ku rei* for power, *sei hei ki* for harmony, *hon sha ze sho* for distant healing, *dai ko myo* the master symbol, and *raku* for completion are easily found with an internet search) visualizing them at the start of your meditation practice or place them in the form of art on walls or in picture frames on tables and shelves. Create your intention board, use inspiring words,

Ésprit with SoZoKi

pictures of places, spaces, and those people you know or wish to bring into your life. Define your mantra, your desires, and particularly your promise to self to remain on this path. Begin and end each session with thanks and gratefulness for the opportunity to commune your Holy Spirit to the Divine with *SoZoKi*.

Define Your Rituals

Every aspect of life, all societies, be it religion, culture, education, athletics, or militia, utilize ritual for a variety of reasons. They are used to provide relief, as in prayer, to maintain and sustain a community or society, to ensure knowledge is imparted and expanded through the generations. Rituals are present in celebrations, inductions...throughout life, from birth to death, filling our existence with sequences of activity that include words, gestures, and objects in a repetitive practice. Rituals can be personal or communal, serving to promote a feeling of protection or cause harm. In your practice of *Ésprit with SoZoKi* you will need to create rituals to support your intention.

To help you get started, I suggest that after reading this section you put this book aside, and take a pencil and paper to task, and that you limit it to an hour.

You want to consider the wide range of activities that should receive your attention in your energy practice rituals. For instance, in our lives we eat and drink, sleep, exercise our body and brain. We also work, play, have sex, reproduce, and create. Perhaps the most dominant activity is that we think. In fact, we think constantly, filtering a myriad of issues, questions, hopes, data points, and innumerable other thoughts that may visit, invite or demand our attention. A person may have 60,000 thoughts in a day, the vast majority of them repetitious from the same and/or the previous day.

Obviously the better you understand how you think, the better will be your selection of thoughts to manage and those you might dismiss, at least for the time being. The more efficient you are in filtering your thoughts, the simpler your life will be.

That said, you would do well to contemplate, through rituals, all the different life-sustaining aspects of your life. See them as sacred, respect them, give them your attention and your energy.

Your energy practice rituals should touch on each of these aspects of your life. You may choose to achieve this through multiple opportunities throughout the day or to practice the majority at one set recurring time.

If you are a negative thinker, start where your thought flows easily. Begin by listing the ideas in your head and then writing them on paper. The negatives might come to mind starting with something like, "I can't .. I don't .. They won't .. I shouldn't. When you write them down, leave a space after it, for you are going to ultimately rewrite that negative statement with a new statement based on a new approach like, "I can .. I do .. They will ... I shall."

The degree of the negativity you have on a particular issue will likely determine how much time it will take for you to reverse your attitude on it. But here is the key. The sooner you catch yourself in a negative, and then think of it again in positive terms, the sooner the negative will go away. Yes, it will take time and practice, and you don't want to beat yourself up about not catching it quickly. The more time you invest in the practice, the more confidence you will have in eradicating the negative.

My practice is to catch myself and speak the alternative six times in a day. After that, I will just notice the negative and give myself a break until tomorrow. You don't have to do six times. Use whatever feels right to you. You may start with a smaller number and that will work on some negatives, or find that you need to catch it more often. You may find that you can start with a higher number and then lower it because you are making progress.

Also, you might limit yourself to a certain number of negatives; maybe start with just one big one or a few little ones. You can tailor the approach based on how you feel about what you face and the progress you feel you are making.

My thought is that it takes a few times to 'get the hang of it' in most everything we do. We need to allow enough thought to occur in one direction so that the change gets as much 'bang for the buck' when making that thought adjustment (TA). If you are running to the start of your day I would not suggest a change to your morning ritual, but rather find time for it in the evening. Eventually the changes made at the end of the day will impact the beginning.

Sleep It's an important ritual and one of the most beneficial health habits we can possess. Everyone requires a different amount, but most need somewhere between seven and eight hours each night. Rare are those who only need 4 hours without negatively impacting their emotional and/or physical health. Naps during the day can mitigate a lack sleep at night, but napping won't fulfill the need for solid sleep.

In the article *The sleep deprived human brain* the researchers suggested sleep deprivation (SD) triggers negative processing of emotions which include anxiety, irritability, emotional instability, aggression, and thoughts of suicide that actually potentiate to attempts and completion. They went on to postulate that sleep deprivation alters the more complex domains of the ability to regulate irritability, emotional expression, and discrimination. [25]

Work How is work going for you? More than 52% of Americans are unhappy with their jobs. [26] Some are more than unhappy, experiencing a physical ailment due to subconscious disdain for the job, a boss, or co-workers. When unemployment is prevalent, many people are "stuck" in their jobs because they can't find an alternative to their current situation. If you are disappointed with your job, career, or lack thereof, find a way to make a change. It may seem easier to say than to do. You may need to relocate, start at a lower position making less money, or have a longer commute. But depending on what you want to leave, and how much negativity it is producing in your life, in the long term it may be best for you. As most in the workforce full-time find themselves spending 80,000 hours over their lifetime on the job, the sooner you can move from a negative to a positive situation the better.

Sexuality Many people think that lust and love are interchangeable, but in truth, sex, reproduction, and lust are all attached to attraction rather than the emotion we call love. Genetic gender tendencies, aka hormones, drive the actual act in a variety of ways. Though it is often denied in many societies and cultures, sexual energy is a natural force. Its existence cannot be denied though it is in many places. What happens when natural sexual energy is not released? Frustration, naturally, and that can lead to depression, angry outbursts, lack of natural energy, excessive eating habits, poor self-esteem, inability to establish adequate sleep habits, and other health problems.

As you explore, acknowledge, and work on these aspects of life, the ability to grow your energy healing abilities for self and others is enhanced and blossoms. Again, change does not occur overnight. You will need to allow and accept an honest self-evaluation. The good news, regardless of any limitations you might identify, is that only you with your spiritual consciousness are involved in this process. You do not need an appointment with a therapist, nor do you need to attend a support group. (That said, I do offer education sessions if you feel you need assistance in developing your practice. Private and group Zoom appointments can be scheduled at www.SoZoKi.com). Continue your religious practice, attend classes that stimulate your mind or body, join in programs that offer volunteer services, if they continue to feel right for you, and not just a habit, but while you continue with them be sure to begin your personal energy healing practice, growing your lively spirit with *SoZoKi*.

Successful Meditation

In Chapter Six of *SoZoKi -- Creation's Energy* (Energy is Energy) I share a variety of meditative methods used around the globe. For those interested in diving deeper into the subject, an Internet search yields a variety of websites and articles to enhance your knowledge. In Chapter 11, I provided a non-guided meditation for those who have not been able to calm their mind to the extent that they are prevented or inhibited from enjoying a successful self-practice. So often our minds are overflowing with the thought traffic about our everyday lives. Attempting to calm this naturally occurring process is often very difficult, with

Ésprit with SoZoKi

frustration resulting in the abandonment of the very idea of meditative practice.

If you have been unable to meditate, despite previous attempts at the practice, I would recommend starting with a simple non-guided type of meditation. You may think you do not have the time to include a daily practice of meditation, but please understand that you do not have to be in a special place, nor do you need to secure a large amount of time, for this approach to increasing your energy flow.

While you may need to invest time in the beginning, meditation or calming your mind will only take a few minutes after you have developed your approach. Practice experience should allow you to identify the time of day when meditation is best for you to enjoy the benefits. And there's this. You should also be able to identify potential conflicts that could be defused with mini-meditative moments. For instance, if you are about to engage in a distasteful task or have an interaction with a difficult person and others???,. Stop, take a few slow, deep cleansing breaths, then purposefully set in your mind your intention for the impact of interaction on you. Remember, you cannot control the outcome of a difficult interaction, but you do have complete control of its

Ésprit with SoZoKi

impact on you. Before you start always set your intention to attach to the natural flow of *SoZoKi*. Personally, I wrap a bubble of *SoZoKi* protection around me whenever I feel or intuit a need, and I've done this for days on end, more than once in this lifetime! I never said life was easy, and why I believe *Ésprit with SoZoKi* is so important to share.

Meditation is an opportunity to remind yourself of your spiritual consciousness. It is an opportunity to connect with the Divine and access *SoZoKi* to grow your awareness of the opportunities for detoxifying and strengthening that exist throughout your day. Like a prayer, meditation is a powerful process, bringing love and respect to yourself so that you can then shower it upon others in your life.

Reinforce Patterns

Understanding and identifying daily mantras to assist you in holding spirit rather than falling back into our human conscious is imperative to successful evolution of your thoughts and actions. What is a mantra or how does a mantra come about? *Mantra* is a word taken from Hinduism with an origin in the part of the *Vedas* (the earliest Hindu scriptures) containing hymns. They began as repetitive truisms from sacred messages and texts,

Ésprit with SoZoKi

or special words used to spark charms and spells when counsel was sought. In 1956, the year of my birth, the use of the word mantra to describe meditation was introduced to the English language as an instrument of thought or an instrument to help us control our thought. Mantras are also the vocalization of a sound, a word, or a series of words that are repeated when practicing meditation to bring calm to the onslaught of thought that engages our mind, and focus to what needs your attention. [27,28]

What are your mantras? If the word isn't new to you, you probably have some already. If it is new, or you've been out of practice using them, retrieve an earlier mantra or choose a new one that better fits who you are today. I need to remind you that repetitive thoughts, both positive and negative, train your brain to think a certain way. A positive mantra can produce endorphins (our happy hormones) and serotonin (our feel good chemical) neuropeptides, but excessive sadness & negative statements we tell ourselves can equally produce corticotropin-releasing hormones found in mood disorders. The important take-away here is our cellular structure modifies to accommodate more of the neuropeptide associated with that emotion. It's a vicious cycle you have to break, if you find yourself experiencing overwhelming emotion for

Ésprit with SoZoKi

an extended period of time.

This is not to say we should not experience sadness. The indigenous peoples of America have an anonymous quote: The soul would have no rainbow if the eyes had no tears. It is when our emotions are out of balance that we begin to see physical manifestations of a negative emotional state of mind. Examples of health-promoting chemical release are positive or pleasant emotions, moods and thoughts, like hope, love, empathy, optimism, confidence, humor, joy, inspiration and acceptance. Shame, guilt, anger, hate, apathy and fear are all examples of health-degrading emotions.

Our thoughts are impacting our health at the structural cellular level throughout our body, clearly identifying our need to proactively engage in strategic patterned use of mantras to sustain a strong flow of *SoZoKi*.

In the United States, we live in a society that doesn't support meditation breaks throughout the course of a day. To promote and sustain thought in the direction of spirituality rather than secularity does not compute within the common practice of capitalism. In other words, the minimal breaks given to a workforce are established for food or drink, smoking, or using a restroom. Breaks are given to produce a good work product, not because

Ésprit with SoZoKi

the capitalist is concerned for the worker's spiritual health, and so are of a limited time to ensure efficiency for business sustainability.

So what is spiritual health? While intrinsically difficult to define or see a healthy spirit in someone, we can see the outcomes on a person's health in increased or decreased emotional, social, and physical capabilities (body). Our ability to achieve communal harmony with all life is possible but is mostly unfamiliar in the American society. Other cultures around the world that are less branded capitalism create more time and space for them to experience, study, and practice better spiritual health cultures.

Here in the United States, we historically tended to limit days off from work to the practice of the most commonly held religions, Christianity and Judaism, e.g., Saturdays or Sundays. By placing capitalist production above spiritual care, with the minimalist approach of once a week to focus on spirit (aka., going to church), we have created a society that is far more focused on what we own rather than who we are. All said, it is left to the individual to develop a health sustaining program that can be scheduled into the workflow of their employer. Understanding your energy body, your spirit's attachment to *SoZoKi* and the practice you

Ésprit with SoZoKi

develop with this knowledge will empower you to keep energy flowing while you work!

Removing Caustic Circumstances & People

We all need nourishment for our body but to give limited break time to feeding the spirit rather than the body does not align with our innate survival instinct. However, we can develop our mantras and weave them throughout our day to level the playing field. You may easily fall victim to negative speech patterns of a co-worker. The day starts out great, but you arrive at the office to a constant rain of complaints, not from your boss, but from an associate. She may not have authority over you but you can't escape her presence, and the day goes downhill from the moment you arrive.

First you must identify the pattern of your behavior. You awoke fine, you enjoyed your morning before going to work, your thoughts were not negative but looking forward to what the day would bring, how you could help, and what you could accomplish. And then another human brings you down into the reality they have created for themselves. This is exactly when your self-practice of *Ésprit with SoZoKi* can help you to survive, if not actually evolve, from this interaction. Your mantra -- words written out on a card, perhaps, or an icon

Ésprit with SoZoKi

that represents the thought -- should be somewhere you can see it upon arrival to your desk, using it to stop the negativity -- maybe even craziness -- before it even starts. Don't listen to the negativity. Deliberately block it from your thoughts. Instead, silently repeat your mantra to stop the tirade before it can even get its hold on you. Share a short and to the point vocal concern like, "I'm sorry you're struggling." Then follow that up by staking out your right to privacy by saying, "I need to address a work issue that was on my mind all night," and begin to focus on work. When people only get their life energy by the interactions they have with another, when they have to engage and pull the other into their thought processes to feel empowered, the best thing for self-preservation is to empower yourself to identify and disengage. Once the other person understands that they no longer will receive from you the attention that they were, consciously or subconsciously, seeking from you, they will stop their behavior because your energy is no longer available to feed them. They have lost you as their emotional energy source, and you have realigned your human consciousness to spirit.

While others are responsible for their behavior, the same is true for you. If you wish to allow yourself to become their victim then by all means continue

Ésprit with SoZoKi

to allow them to lower your spirit to feed their human drama. On the other hand, if you desire to own yourself and stop an intended or unintended assault on your spirit, then you must own your own behavior.

As you can see with this example, it is not merely finding a few words to repeat continuously to yourself. You first have to identify the structure, timing, and content of the interaction that brings you down. Secondly, you need to find the correct words that will interrupt their behavior and restore your connection with your spirit. And third, you must have an action plan to inhibit their ability to overpower your spirit and bring you down into the mud with their personal struggle.

Inviting Energy of the Spirit

As with any practice you need to begin with setting your intention. This could also be called a prayer; reciting it in your mind or out loud. I mentioned in the introduction to Chapter 6 in *SoZoKi / Creation's Energy* that a shaman prayer used by a massage therapist produced the same energy I had only associated with the practice of Reiki. Consider this mantra as you begin your practice:

Allow Creation's Energy to Manifest and

Ésprit with SoZoKi

Sustain Light, Love, and Truth in My Life Today and Every Day

If it inspires you, modify it if you like, and incorporate it into your thought processes throughout each day.

Shamanism offers guidance in successful praying which includes staying present, as if your objective is already realized. Pray from your heart with intense emotion to infuse your prayer or intention into your reality. Use with precision the words you choose, make them clear and unequivocal. Affirm your trust in the Holy Spirit, leaving no room for doubt.

Make use of the words "I Am" and focus on a point within your heart. Rhyme, rhythm, and repetition produce a deep influence that inspires and luminates the power of your prayer. Have a clear vision with firm intention to achieve powerful results. Spend some time in meditation or quiet contemplation after your prayer to listen and anticipate inspired thought. Finally, complete the prayer and meditation with an action that supports and allows your request to manifest.

There is a wide variety of approach to prayer influenced by perceptions which are sometimes antagonistic. The way a person sees their world with factors including politics, culture, race, and creed influences how they pray. One may pray for

Ésprit with SoZoKi

their enemy to be killed, another may ask to be forgiven or saved. Some pray for abundance, while others become angry with the Divine because they feel powerless in a difficult life, feeling ignored in the face of their belief they are known to God. Many are thankful, praising God for the love they feel, acknowledging how wonderful God is, and identifying themselves as a reflection of the Almighty, seeking God's will to be done. [29]

These varying approaches to prayer remind me of two models used in healthcare and beyond. The first is the Kubler-Ross model, introduced in the 1950s, and known as the five stages of grief. Initially introduced as the observed stages of a person diagnosed with a terminal illness, they include denial, anger, bargaining, depression and acceptance. [30]

The second model is Maslow's hierarchy of needs, introduced to the field of psychology in the 1940s. In this model, Maslow identified the stages of psychological growth. At the bottom of the pyramid, the base is to meet our physiological needs of homeostasis, food, water, sleep, and shelter. After these foundational needs have been met, our psychological focus is on safety and includes personal security, financial security, and health or well-being. Once met, we move upward

Ésprit with SoZoKi

to esteem, seeking to sustain our ego through status, wanting recognition, respect, self-confidence, strength, independence, and freedom. Next we reach for self-actualization, acquiring a mate, creating and parenting offspring, using our abilities and talents, pursuing goals and seeking happiness. Finally, we move beyond self-actualization into self-transcendence with the realization of a desire beyond self, becoming altruistic, spiritual, relating to others human to human, as well as other species and nature. [31.]

Awareness of these two models of human behavior helps us identify how we and others are experiencing life. They provide frameworks of human tendencies that well may influence the difference in how we pray. If you prefer a prayer that has always held significance in your life, then recite it rather than any of the ones provided here. I would also recommend you spend some time on a Google search, seeking the intention that rings true to you. The following are intentions taught in the *Usui Shiki Ryoho*.

Ésprit with SoZoKi

<u>The Reiki Ideals</u>
Just for today, I will let go of anger.
Just for today, I will let go of worry.
Just for today I will give thanks for my many blessings.
Just for today, I will do my work honestly.
Just for today, I will be kind to myself, my neighbor and every living thing. [32.]

<u>The Great Invocation</u>
From the point of Light within the Mind of God
Let light stream forth into the minds of men.
Let Light descend on Earth.

From the point of Love within the Heart of God
Let love stream forth into the hearts of men.
May Love return to Earth

From the center where the Will of God is known
Let purpose guide the little wills of men -

Ésprit with SoZoKi

The purpose which the masters know and serve

From the center which we call the race of men
Let the Plan of Love and Light work out
And may it seal the door where evil dwells.

Let Light and Love and Power restore the Peace on Earth. [33.]

Shaman White Light of Protection Prayer

Great Spirit:

I call upon the white light of protection

to come forth from the golden orb above my head,

covering my entire body from the top of my head to the bottom of my feet,

through each chakra extending through my entire aura.

This light surrounds, protects, heals and guides me,

Going within to further protect, cleanse, purify and heal,

Ésprit with SoZoKi

Totally permeating my entire being.

I ask that any and all negative, sickly, jealous, evil, or mean
energies, entities, spirits, guides, or vibrations that have attached themselves to me be sent back to their source,
never to return.

I ask this blessing with neither love nor hate, but for sake of the greatest good.

I thank you. [34.]

The Shaman's Prayer

I am already given to the power that rules my fate.

I cling to nothing, so I have nothing to defend.

I have no thoughts, so I will See.

I fear nothing, so I will remember myself.

Detached and at ease, I will dart past the Eagle
To be free. [35.]

Ésprit with SoZoKi

Feet & Hand Chakras

There are a myriad minor chakras throughout the body, and each carries the same characteristics of the seven majors. They appear as little cyclones; each is a little whirling energy vortex, and exists where joints are located. Examples include within the hands and feet as well as the shoulders, elbows, wrists, hips and knees. They are also located where nerve plexuses or bundles exist throughout the body.

Dysfunction of the secondary chakras can have a detrimental impact on the entire chakra system. Connective tissue has a primary responsibility for carrying electromagnetic energy and much of it is located in our buttocks and legs. When cut off below the hips almost 40% of natural energy that feeds vital internal organs can result in a diminished life force that carries us through each day.

In our American culture we tend to identify ourselves as highly intellectual, giving importance to the upper part of our body over the lower part, often thinking we are *a cut above* those with less intellect. With this thought comes the potential to cut off energy flow in our legs resulting in dysfunction. Sluggish bodies and sleepy heads produce confusion, depression, and frustration with our inability to establish a balanced mind-body-spirit

Ésprit with SoZoKi

quality.

If you have this approach to being, you may not be able to use your feet to ground your spirit to readily available Earth energy and then guide it up your legs, through your hips, and into your root chakra, opening the vortex for *SoZoKi* to freely flow. Regard to self and world views has significant impact on your ethereal body. To rethink the importance you have placed solely on intellect as an asset that makes you superior, is to recognize the imbalance the whole suffers when this idea reigns.

Feet chakras are primarily used to bring energy into your ethereal body. Most guided meditations have you visualize growing roots from your feet that move past the layers of the floor through the foundation of the building, sending them deep into the Earth to attach the spirit to an abundance of available energy. In the *SoZoKi* meditation and self-practice, the feet chakras are used to ground the spirit lightly to earth energy before sending it out to Creation. Roots are sent from the feet across a large plot of earth, spreading shallowly instead of growing deep. Energy is pulled from the earth, but the majority of energy is brought in from infinite *SoZoKi* rather than finite earth.

Hand chakras are associated with the upper three

Ésprit with SoZoKi

chakras - Throat, Third Eye, and Crown - and while filled with mini chakras at the many joints, they have one larger located in the center of the palm. Because of the number of chakras, energy flow is not limited to the palm, with each finger transmitting energy at levels associated with colors. Red is traditionally channeled from the index finger and thumb (Root), green from the middle (Heart), blue from the ring (Throat), and violet from the small (Crown). When energy vibrates it produces color, and for those with the ability to see aura, they are seeing the ethereal body or energy fields of life. The energy flow that produces the colors are influenced by the status of the upper chakras, as well as physical limitations of the neck and shoulders. A stiff neck can reduce the energy in the hands, as well as the colors emanating from the fingers.

NB: FYI I do not see auras, but I do know energy vibrates to produce different colors, depending upon the vibration - Violet light has the highest energy, frequency and vibration and the shortest wavelength of visible light.

The points of meridian included within the distal forearm, wrist, and thumb are associated with specific organs in acupuncture therapy. LI4 is located in the thumb joint and is associated with

Ésprit with SoZoKi

the large intestine. LU 7 and 9 are located at the wrist and distal forearm respectively, on the thumb side and is associated with the heart. Finally, HC6 & 7 are located mid distal forearm, mid wrist, and the side of the little finger. These points are associated with the heart pericardium, the thin soft tissue layer that encases the heart. [36.]

Associated with the acts of giving and receiving, the hand chakras are used to channel energy to heal another as well as bring energy for self-healing. Signs of healthy and open hand chakras include openness, confidence, and creativity. When you feel numb or closed off, you may experience a lack of creativity or be unable to express yourself artistically. When you feel unconnected to those in your world or the world at large, this can also be a symptom of closed hand chakras, which diminish the entry of *SoZoKi* into your ethereal body, and negate success in channeling to another, or bringing energy in to heal yourself.

Not to worry; there are things you can do to help your hand chakras. Creating art is not limited to those with natural artistic talents. Everywhere you look you can now find adult coloring books, be they in a traditional format of paper and colored pencil or marker, or in free electronic apps. Other opportunities might be to take a sculpting class or

Ésprit with SoZoKi

learn to throw mud. You may like working with wood, creating ceramic pieces, or creative cooking.

A self-healing practice of Reiki can also open your hand chakras. The more you practice, the more they will open. Resting your hands in a bowl of water while you visualize the chakras open (or opening) is another opportunity readily available to most.

A good way for you to feel energy is an exercise called pumping Ki (key) or Chi (chee). In a sitting position bring your hands to chest level with palms facing each other and about 4 inches apart. Begin moving your hands closer to each other, maybe an inch, and then back to the original space between. The motion is fairly rapid, similar to the rate of chest compressions during CPR. After you get a feel for the movement, close your eyes and continue the hand movement. Now that you have removed visual stimuli focus on the space between your palms. You should begin to sense the creation of a ball as you move hands toward each other and a resistance like a stretching a rubber band as you move the hands away from each other. Once you begin to feel this, slow the motion of your hands down so that you can feel the full effect of the energy you have created.

Some practitioners recommend rubbing your

Ésprit with SoZoKi

palms together to open the chakras. I was not taught this method and would suggest that you not follow this guidance. When you rub your hands too hard for too long you create heat and provide a false sense of energy flow. Most will describe energy flow from the hands as feeling like a heating pad being placed upon them. This does not help yourself nor another as the heat being felt was generated by vigorous rubbing which created friction and resulted in surface heat.

Ésprit with SoZoKi

10 - Hand Positions
(Pushing and Pulling Energy)

The polarity of the hands and feet chakras are both positive, pulling earth energy (feet) and *SoZoKi* (hands) into the ethereal body for self-healing. The positive polarity of the Root chakra pulling *SoZoKi*, as well as its indirect pull of Earth energy from grounded feet chakras, results in a powerhouse energy vortex that allows maximum entry of energy into our ethereal body. There is a variety of approach to your sessions, and it is determined by your need or intent. If you are treating an injured area to assist with healing you will place cupped hands over the injury and focus your intention to increase *SoZoKi* through feet and Root Chakra, visualize it moving up to the chakra located or associated with the injured site, and then to the injury. If your intention is to help with a cold or virus, your intention is not to kill but to lift and assist it out of your physical body. When your intention is to cleanse or open blocked chakras with hand placement, you will begin with the Root, working your way up the chakra system. With this approach, your feet will remain positive in polarity, pulling energy from the Earth, and your hands will become negative with intention to access *SoZo-Ki* and push it from your hands into the chakra.

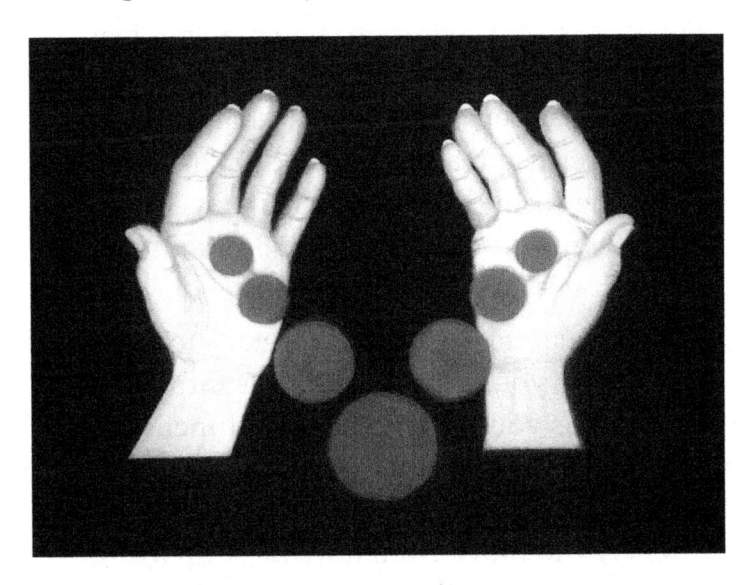

"If You Could See" (2018)

Self-healing hand positions always begin with setting your intention either with use of a prayer (of any faith), those previously provided, or an acknowledging thought for those who are not comfortable with a prayer. You can sit, lay down, or stand; just ensure you are comfortable so that your focus is on energy rather than an uncomfortable position. For all positions, your hands are slightly cupped, palms facing the body.

There is not a set amount of time to spend on a chakra, but my experience is that it can take a few minutes for energy to begin flowing. For me, and this is not true for everyone, my palms turn red and have a very hot sensation. You may not feel heat to begin with, it may happen the first time, or it may never happen. Also, when I channel energy, my closed eyes begin a movement similar to what occurs during REM sleep, so if it happens don't be concerned. I recommend allowing 30-45 minutes for a full self-energy session.

In previous chapters, I provided details for each of the chakras. As you move your hands through the positions, focus your attention on the function of the chakra. For each hand position, set the intention for *SoZoKi* to enter the chakra and then for the energy to move from it to the supporting structures and organs that are associated with it. With your mind's eye, visualize the color of the chakra and see the swirl of energy moving into and then out of the vortex.

Ésprit with SoZoKi

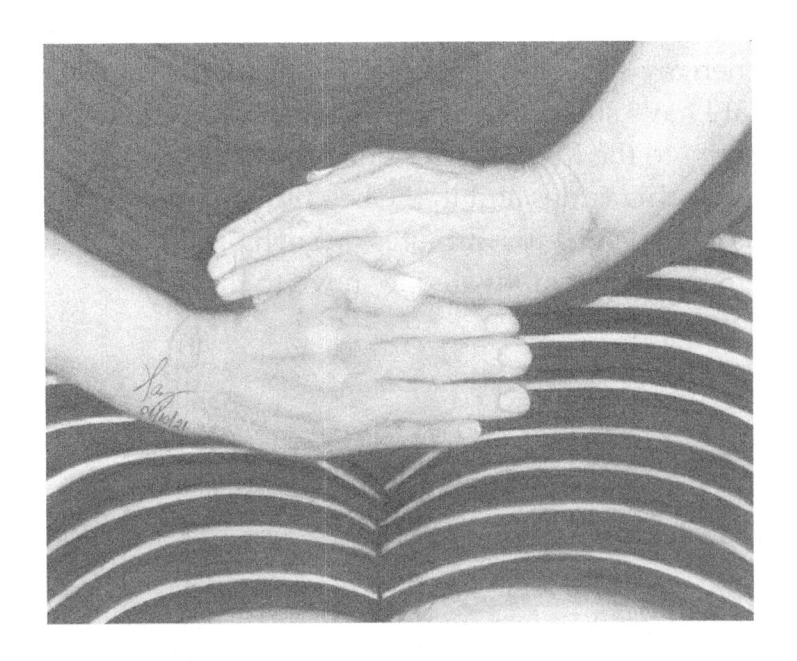

"Root Chakra Hand Position" (2021)

The first-hand position with *SoZoKi* begins with the Root Chakra and can be performed while standing, sitting, kneeling or lying down. The drawing shows the hands slightly cupped with palms facing the area between the top of your thighs, touching the little finger side of one hand to the thumb side of the other. The most important aspect for this position is that the cupped hands hover about 4 to 6 inches above your physical body, and not touching it. Refer to the Root Chakra Hand Position illustration above. For the remaining chakras you can rest your cupped hands on your body.

Ésprit with SoZoKi

When my eyes stop their rapid movement, or I feel that I have succeeded with my intention to channel energy to the Root, I move on to the next position. Again, this varies and in the beginning you may want to spend 4 to 5 minutes on each position before you feel motivated to move to the next chakra.

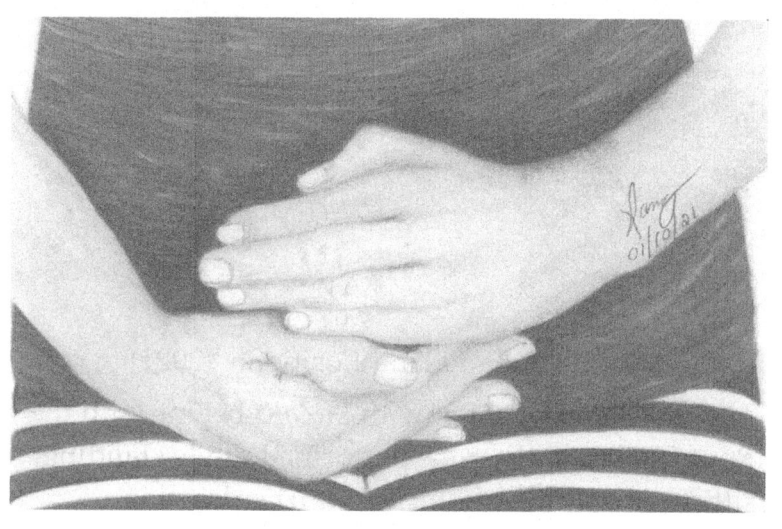

"Sacral Chakra Hand Position" (2021)

The second-hand position is on or above the Sacral Chakra, located just above the pubic bone and below the umbilicus (bellybutton, naval), with hands in the same position as used for the root. Again, hold the position for 4 to 5 minutes or until you are motivated to move to the next chakra.

Ésprit with SoZoKi

"Solar Plexus Hand Position" (2021)

The Solar Plexus is located just above the umbilicus and below the diaphragm, which is the connective tissue that separates the chest and abdominal cavities. This energy vortex, along with the Heart Chakra, is fired up by the increased energy moving along the diaphragm when both chakras are fully functioning. This gives the extra energy needed to change from judgement to opinion and to forgive for our better self. Again, hold the position for 4 to 5 minutes or until you are motivated to move to the next chakra.

In all three of the described positions, the hands hover or are placed directly over the three lower chakras.

Ésprit with SoZoKi

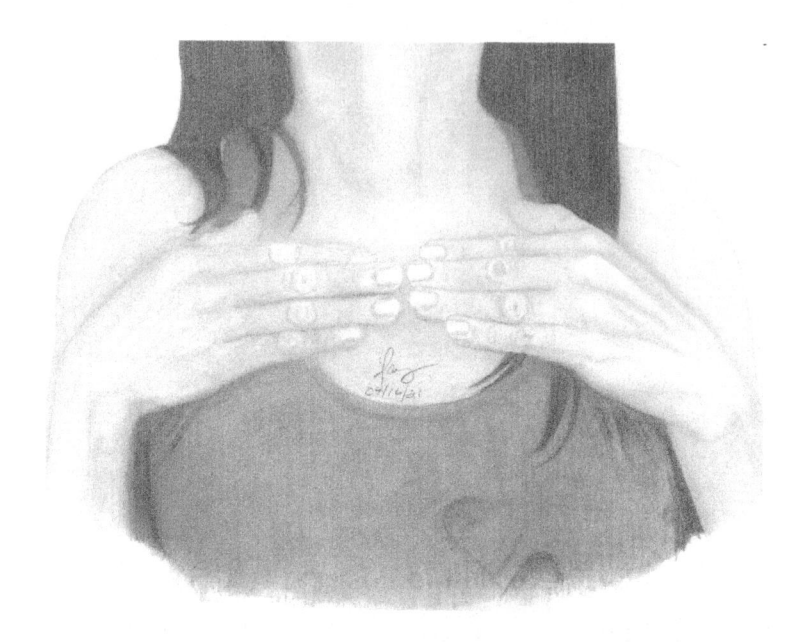

"Heart Chakra Hand Position" (2021)

The Heart Chakra is located mid-sternum (breastbone) and it is not recommended to place your hands directly over this energy vortex. This chakra requires you separate your hands, which are placed to the right and left above the nipple line, in a cupped position, either touching or hovering over your body. Again, hold the position for 4 to 5 minutes or until you are motivated to move to the next chakra.

Ésprit with SoZoKi

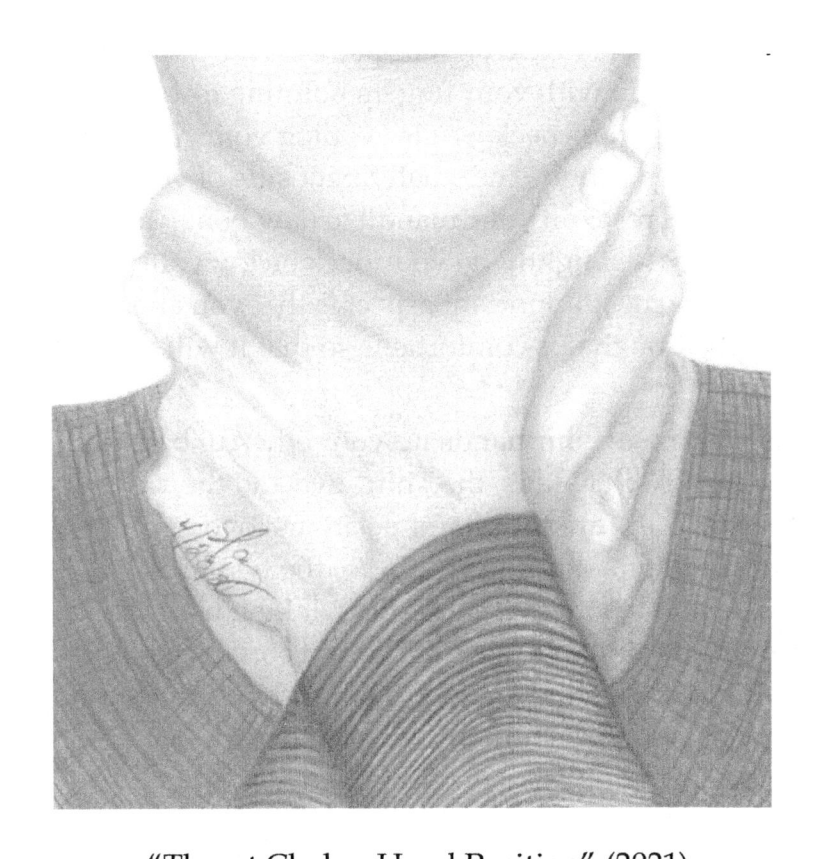

"Throat Chakra Hand Position" (2021)

With the Throat Chakra, located below the chin and above the clavicles (collarbones), in the anterior mid-neck region, your hands will return together in a cupped position as used in the three lower chakras. If you have a short neck you may need to modify the traditional position to accommodate your anatomy. Touch the inside of

Ésprit with SoZoKi

your wrists and base of your palms, over the center of your neck, with your fingers pointing toward the back of your neck, while keeping your hands in a cupped position. The small finger side of your hand will reset on your mandible (jaw bone) and fingertips rest lightly on your neck below your ears. The most important aspect is that you choose the position that is comfortable so that it will work best for you.

As you move your hands up your ethereal body to the final two chakras, the Third Eye and the Crown, there are four hand positions to focus your *SoZoKi* intention upon. These are the two most existential of our energy vortices, taking us to understanding our place in life and connecting our spirit to the Divine. Our human conscious intention is to rise to spirit consciousness so that we may commune with *SoZoKi*.

Ésprit with SoZoKi

When you move up to the Third Eye Chakra, you should separate your hands again and put one over each eye.

"Third Eye and Crown Chakras" (2021)
First Hand Position

Ésprit with SoZoKi

From the neck you will move your hands up with one cupped hand covering each eye. As with all other chakras, you will remain in this position for 3-4 minutes or until you feel prompted to move on.

Next move your cupped hands to cover each ear, resting the tips above ears and base of palms below.

"Third Eye and Crown Chakras" (2021)
Second Hand Position

Ésprit with SoZoKi

After 3-4 minutes, or feel prompted, move your hands to the top of your head. Hands return to the touching cupped position used for the lower chakras.

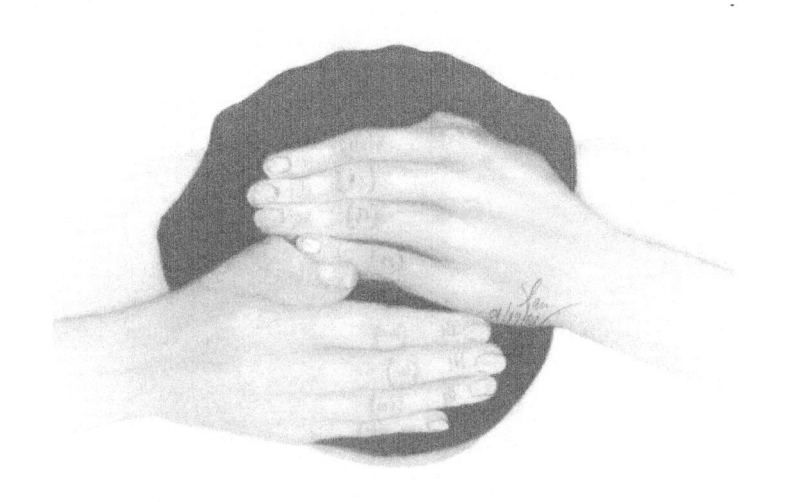

"Third Eye and Crown Chakras" (2021)
Third Hand Position

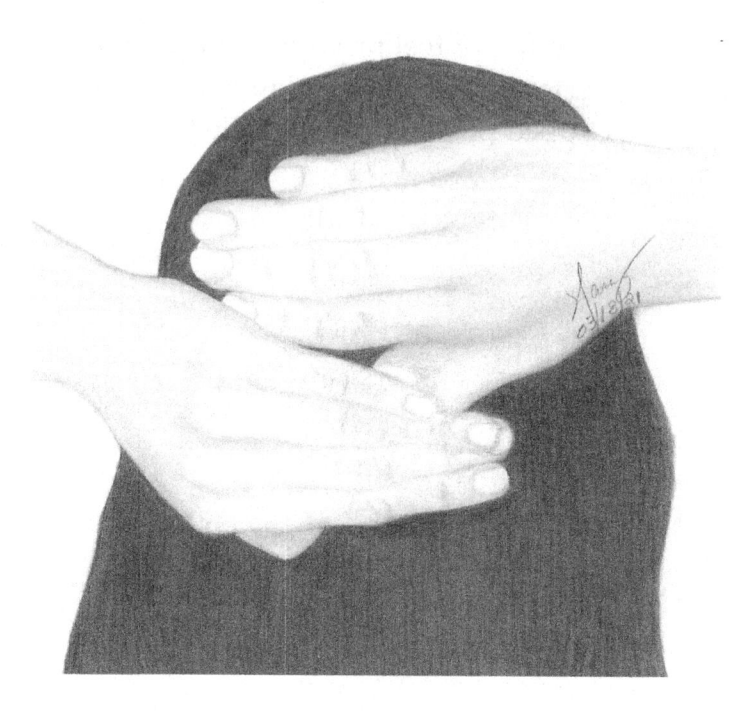

Ésprit with SoZoKi

"Third Eye and Crown Chakras" (2021)
Fourth Hand Position

The final hand position is behind your head and will complete a full energy body self-practice session. After 3-4 minutes or when prompted to move your hands away from the position, allow your hands to rest in your lap or by your sides.

Take a moment to set your intention to carry the energy flow and awareness of your energy body through your day or week. The frequency of your sessions, early in your practice, will impact the outcome you may be seeking. As with anything in life, at least it's been my experience, the more time you spend the better you become.

NB: Hint, hint - have you checked out my art? www.OriginalDNA.com I didn't start drawing until December 2000 - I have not had a lesson from a human but was certainly guided, as I continue to be, by my Spirit with SoZoKi.

Ésprit with SoZoKi

"Filled with Positive and Negative Polarity" (2021)

You will not always have time or need to complete a full body energy session. Sometimes you may only want to set your intention and focus on a particular spot, like a sore knee, hip, foot, elbow or shoulder. Other times you may wish to use *SoZoKi* to help you clear your mind so that you can fall

Ésprit with SoZoKi

asleep. When I use *SoZoKi* to calm my mind to sleep, I start with the Crown positions and move down the chakras. Typically I fall asleep by the time my hands have moved to my chest in the heart chakra position. I have found great success with playing a soft meditation music recording while my hands move through the positions.

Should you desire to learn more, have the need for interactive learning, prefer private or group (up to 6 people), you can now reserve sessions with me at www.SoZoKi.com or scan this barcode with your smartphone.

Ésprit with SoZoKi

11 - *Ésprit Energy Meditations*

Many if not most guided meditations I have participated in have been focused on grounding the listener to Earth energy. I see nothing wrong with this approach, but I believe it is essential to offer an additional mode to calm the mind while invoking Creation's love. The Earth offers incredible energy to support all that dwells on it. However, there exists much more than our little blue planet. Powerful as its energy is, it is a part of Creation, so why not reach beyond the limitations of Earth, beyond our solar system, beyond our universe and request the support of all of Creation? The following are two meditations designed to access Creation's limitless energy.

<u>Non-Guided Meditation</u>

For those who prefer a non-guided meditation I recommend the following, especially if you are a beginner or have had difficulty in the past in

Ésprit with SoZoKi

calming your mind. You will need the following: an unscented candle, a comfortable seating arrangement, turn the phone, television, and music off, ensure pets/family are in a part of your home where they will not interrupt you for at least 15 minutes and use a room that you can completely darken. The idea is to remove all external stimuli except the candle you will light.

Once you are comfortable, have lit the candle and removed all other stimuli you will begin a rolling breath technique. You many need to start at a slow count of 4 and work your way up to 8, or you might have great breathing already and can count to 8 without difficulty. The idea is to begin a slow inhale through your nose, filling the lower lobes of your lungs and then filling them to capacity. Just as you have reached capacity there is a very brief pause before you begin to exhale slowly through your mouth. If you have difficulty breathing through your nose don't worry, you can use only your mouth and still get the same outcome. Purposeful breathing is what you are trying to train yourself to do as we rarely think about breathing unless we can't do it.

If you can do no more than a count of 4 you will begin filling your lungs mentally counting to 4 and then count again to 4 on the exhale. At the end of

Ésprit with SoZoKi

inhale and exhale is a very brief pause. This is the rolling breath technique. Eventually with practice you will increase your capacity to 8 and will also no longer need to count as you have trained your body to the process.

After you have successfully created your breathing technique you will then move your focus from your breathing to the flickering flame of the candle. You can practice this while you are in breath training so that when you no longer need to count you will be able to relax your mind. Allow the flame to transition your mind into what it referred to as a Beta Mind State or the subconscious overpowering the conscious mind.

The following guided mediation will be available on YouTube later in 2021 for those seeking an internally guided experience. Here I have provided the narrative and once learned you can use music and/ or visual media to enhance the experience. Regardless of your approach it is always best that you are not going to be interrupted by life and you are in a very comfortable position and climate.

Guided Ésprit Meditation

Begin the *Ésprit with SoZoKi* meditation with 6 rolling breaths. Slowly begin inhaling through your nose, filling the lower lobes of your lungs. As the

Ésprit with SoZoKi

space is filled complete the inhale by filling your upper lungs to capacity. Briefly pause and begin to exhale through your mouth, slowly allowing the air to escape out of your upper lungs, then mildly push the remaining air out of your lower lungs. Breath in through your nose filling the lower and then upper lungs to capacity. After a brief pause, slowly exhale, allowing the air to escape out of your upper lungs, then mildly push the remaining air out of your lower lungs. Breath in through your nose filling the lower and then upper lungs to capacity. After a brief pause, slowly exhale, allowing the air to escape out of your upper lungs, then mildly push the remaining air out of your lower lungs. Breath in through your nose, filling the lower and then the upper lobes of the lungs to capacity. After a brief pause, slowly exhale, allowing the air to escape out of your upper lungs, then mildly push the remaining air out of your lower lungs. Again, breath in through your nose filling the lower lobes of your lungs and then upper lobes to capacity. Pause briefly and then slowly exhale, allowing the air to escape out of your upper lungs, then mildly push the remaining air out of your lower lungs. Last time, breath in through your nose filling the lower and then upper lobes of your lungs to capacity. After a brief pause, slowly exhale, allowing the air to escape out of

Ésprit with SoZoKi

your upper lungs, then mildly push the remaining air out of your lower lungs.

Return to your natural breathing pattern and begin to visualize the Root Chakra, swirling below the trunk of the body, before it attaches to the base of your spine. The Root Chakra is associated with the element earth, the color red, and the scent of cinnamon. Visualize yourself in nature on the last warm day of fall, toes buried in the soil and surrounded by vivid red leaves while drinking warm apple cider spiced with cinnamon. As you breathe, the Root Chakra opens, allowing an increase of *SoZoKi* to enter your ethereal body. The Root is the chakra of inspiration, and as inspired thought enters your conscious mind through the root, it feeds the remaining chakras located within your ethereal body.

Continue breathing, in through your nose and out through your mouth. Visualize the minor chakras in your feet opening, allowing your energy to flow across the earth, slightly entering the soil. Bring to your mind's eye a beautiful, lush weeping willow tree. Ground your spirit energy, as roots of the willow, just below the surface. Lightly attach your spirit to earth before sending it up and out to all of creation, past the clear blue sky, moving through the stars of the Milky Way, beyond this universe

Ésprit with SoZoKi

and into all that is exists. Request *SoZoKi* to enter your ethereal body through the Root and minor chakras of your hands while your feet chakras keep your spirit grounded to earth.

Continue breathing and bring your focus up to the Sacral Chakra, located just below your navel, guiding *SoZoKi* up from the Root and into this chakra. The sacral chakra is associated with the element water, the color orange, and the scent of dragon's blood. Orange symbolizes energy, excitement, vitality, and good health. Sacral is the chakra of intuition of the inspired thought that entered through the Root. Still in nature during the fall season, visualize yourself sitting on a rock with your feet in a pool of water. As you continue to breathe, light a dragon's blood incense stick, filling your being with the scent as you are drenched in the color of orange leaves dancing in the breeze of a cool fall day.

As *SoZoKi* is pulled upward to enter the Solar Plexus, acknowledge the inspired thought that entered through the Root and was intuited in the Sacral chakras, entering the Solar Plexus for an opinion or judgement to be formed. The element associated with this chakra is fire, the color is yellow, and the scent is ginger. Continue to visualize yourself in nature, sitting by a fire, and as the yellow flames

Ésprit with SoZoKi

dance, breathe in the scent of ginger from the plants that surround you.

As you visualize *SoZoKi* being pushed from the Solar Plexus up and into your Heart Chakra located in the middle of your breastbone continue to allow your natural breathing pattern. Envision *SoZoKi* carrying the opinion or judgement formed in the Solar Plexus into your heart chakra and seize the opportunity to re-consider if needed. The element associated with the Heart Chakra is air, the color is green, and the scent is rose. Remaining in nature visualize yourself walking into a rose garden as your bare feet sink into a lush green lawn. Breath in the fresh air to smell the sweet scent of the roses as you focus on re-consideration of judgments and opinions.

As *SoZoKi* continues its upward movement it is pushed from the Heart and pulled into the Throat, the chakra of communication. Inspired thought has been intuited and judged in the lower chakras, moved into the upper heart chakra where it has been reconsidered before it enters the Throat where it is vocalized to the world. The element associated with the Throat Chakra is ether, the clear sky, the heavens. The color associated with this chakra is blue, and the scent is sandalwood. Visualize yourself walking out of the rose garden and into a

Ésprit with SoZoKi

lush green field. As you lay down in the field, your eyes are drenched in the color of a clear blue sky while you breathe in the scent of sandalwood. Continue to breathe in through your nose, and then gently releasing your breath out of your mouth.

In its ever upward movement, *SoZoKi* is pulled out of the throat and into the Third Eye Chakra, the chakra of understanding your place in creation. With *SoZoKi* you have experienced inspired thought, intuited then formed an opinion or made a judgement, and reconsidered before vocalizing to the world. As *SoZoKi* enters the Third Eye you see yourself as a part of, rather than separate from, all that exists. Not above, not below, but in perfect unison with creation, giving you the clairvoyant ability to see with this chakra what you cannot with eyes. The element associated with the Third Eye is light, the color is indigo, and the scent is lavender. After soaking up the blue sky, visualize yourself leaving the green field as you enter a new one abundant with lavender and wild indigo flowers. As you stand in the field sunshine falls gently upon your head while you are surrounded with the color indigo as you breathe in the sweet floral scent of lavender that fills the air. Continue your natural breathing pattern, in through your nose and then gently escaping out of your mouth.

Ésprit with SoZoKi

From the Third Eye, *SoZoKi* leaves the body, moving upward to enter the Crown, the chakra of enlightenment. Having confirmed your place in creation, you now connect to the Divine, Holy Spirit to Holy Spirit, allowing *SoZoKi* to exit your ethereal body, return to creation and then re-enter though the root in the eternal communion of human and spiritual consciousness. The element associated with the Crown Chakra is thought. Attaching your Holy Spirit to God Spirit, your thoughts are drenched in white or violet light as you continue your walk and arrive in a field of wild jasmine. Once released from the Crown, *SoZoKi* enters the Root sustaining a continuous flow to fill, sustain, inspire, and guide your consciousness, attaching human to spirit.

When you are ready bring your spirit fully back into your human consciousness. Wiggle your fingers and toes. Take a deep breath in through your nose then allow it to move out of your lungs through your mouth. Slowly open your eyes. Take this moment to reflect on yourself, the experience of communing with the Divine through the help of *SoZoKi* and give thanks for the opportunity to have lifted your spirit with Creation and The Creator.

Consider finishing your mediation with this mantra:

Ésprit with SoZoKi

Allow creation's energy to manifest and sustain light, love and truth in my life, today and every day.

Ésprit with SoZoKi

To Your Good Health

Thank you for your valuable time spent with this course. Traditional Reiki classes consist of one 8-hour seminar for each the three levels attained. It is my sincere hope that you benefit from the time you have invested and will invest in your *Ésprit with SoZoKi* practice, and that you will share your practice experience. Should you feel or intuit helping another with energy, there is no reason why you should not succeed, but I do request you do not charge anyone for your service. *SoZoKi* can be integrated into your work, but as I have always done, it is a practice of the spirit and should remain a gratuitous action.

Ésprit with SoZoKi

Test Questions

1. A chakra is:
   a. an anatomical structure identified by a bundle of nerves
   b. a yoga position
   c. a swirling conical vortex in the body's ethereal energy field
   d. an anatomical structure where ligaments attach bones to form a joint

2. There are seven major chakras, each located where 21 lines of meridian, or energy highways cross.
   a. True
   b. False

3. A healthy and functioning chakra
   a. promotes inspiration
   b. promotes intuition
   c. influences judgments and opinions
   d. all of the above

Ésprit with SoZoKi

4. Reiki, two Japanese words translating to universal energy, is a finite practice established by Dr. Usui. *SoZoKi*, is two Japanese words combined and translates to _____ _____.
   a. zero energy
   b. abundant energy
   c. lively energy
   d. Creation energy

5. A fundamental ideological difference between Reiki and *SoZoKi*
   a. there is no difference between the practices
   b. only those attuned can practice *SoZoKi*
   c. anyone who is aware and has desire can access *SoZoKi*
   d. only a Reiki Master can access *SoZoKi*

6. *SoZoKi* is a conscious effort to pull earth or universe energy rather than a practice to support a continuous subconscious flow of energy into our ethereal body.
   a. True
   b. False

Ésprit with SoZoKi

7. Which of the following statements about the Root Chakra are correct:
1. It is the second energy vortex in the chakra system
2. The prime functions of the Root Chakra are grounding, security and survival
3. The adrenals are the glands that drive this chakra due to their production of sex hormones rather than their location in the body.
4. The Root Chakra is identified as having masculine or yang properties and is identified as the vortex most closely connected to primal energy and the survival instinct.
   a. 1, 3, 4
   b. 1, 2, 4
   c. 2, 3, 4
   d. All of the above

8. A blocked or dysfunctional Root Chakra can be associated with a high rate of occurrence of:
   a. Elimination complication
   b. Infertility
   c. Psychosocial disorders
   d. None of the above
   e. All of the above

Ésprit with SoZoKi

9. The Root Chakra has a negative polarity, pushing energy into the ethereal body and then pulling it upward so that it will enter the Sacral Chakra.
    a. True
    b. False

10. Which of the following statements is incorrect regarding foods that support an open and healthy Root Chakra include:
1. No food as fasting best supports the health of the root chakra.
2. Proteins including meats, eggs, nuts, and beans support the health of the root chakra.
3. Vegetables grown within the earth, such as potatoes, sweet potatoes, turnips, carrots, onion, garlic, ginger, and turmeric support the health of the root chakra.
4. Tomatoes, strawberries, raspberries, cherries, pomegranates, and apples, will support the health of the root chakra.
    a. 3
    b. 4
    c. 2
    d. 1

11. The governance of relationships and emotions is associated with which chakra?
    a. Sacral
    b. Heart
    c. Root
    d. Solar Plexus

12. One of the highest expressions of a healthy Sacral Chakra:
    a. We experience intuitive understanding in our intimate relationships.
    b. We understand that allowance of freedom to individuate in a partnership results in a relationship unencumbered by fear of loss.
    c. We are sensitive in our relationships.
    d. All of the above.

13. When this chakra is blocked it can manifest as illness, depleting or depressing our natural immune response.
    a. Throat
    b. Sacral
    c. Heart
    d. Crown

Ésprit with SoZoKi

14. This chakra is also associated with our creative life. When it is healthy, we have a sense of "feeling alive" and creativity flows. When blocked, we experience frustration in our creative process or even lose the ability to be creative:
    a. Root
    b. Third Eye
    c. Sacral
    d. Crown

15. Eastern cultures believe opposites should coexist in an interdependence with self, defined by obligations and relations. Western thought processes isolate and objectify with an idea of an independent self in their intra-personal interactions.
    a. True
    b. False

16. Orange is the color associated with the Sacral Chakra. To support energy flow through this chakra which foods you should include in your diet?
    a. sweet potatoes, yams, mangos
    b. oranges, peaches, apricots, orange peppers, and carrots
    c. salmon, sardines, oysters, olives, eggs, navy beans
    d. chia seeds, soybeans, Brussel sprouts, and canola oil
    e. all of the above

17. The sense associated with the Sacral Chakra is _____ and the color is _____.
    a. Sight, blue
    b. Taste, yellow
    c. Taste, orange
    d. Touch, orange

18. To help heal this chakra, during a full moon, find a comfortable place in nature near a body of water -- a creek, lake, ocean or even a pool if none of the others are readily available to you.
    a. Third Eye
    b. Throat
    c. Heart
    d. Sacral

Ésprit with SoZoKi

19. Inspiration occurring in the Root Chakra gives rise to intuition in the Sacral Chakra. What occurs next in the Solar Plexus?
    a. Remorse
    b. Judgment/Opinion
    c. Communication
    d. Forgiveness

20. When the Solar Plexus energy flow is diminished or obstructed, we experience:
1. falling victim to selfishness
2. lack of personal authority
3. seeking power through the control of others
4. feeling empowered
    a. 1,3,4
    b. 2,3,4
    c. 1,2,4
    d. 1,2,3

21. Organ connections to the Solar Plexus Chakra include the stomach, gallbladder, liver and small intestine, and in particular, the pancreas.
    a. True
    b. False

22. Which of the following statements about the Solar Plexus is incorrect:
   a. coordinates energy, vitality and willpower with our desires
   b. considered our body's battery
   c. the divine principle of this chakra is to control others
   d. when blocked or diminished, we have a sense of purposeless existence

23. This chakra is dominated by neither property but exists as the same energy vortex in females and males and is subject to a melting-pot of emotions, both positive and negative.
   a. Root
   b. Solar Plexus
   c. Third Eye
   d. Throat

24. In a *Digestive Diseases and Science* research article published on NCBI in 2014, the authors noted a steady rise in the rate of occurrence of gasrtro-esophageal reflux disease (GERD) around the globe in industrialized countries.
   a. True
   b. False

25. Yoga poses, including planking and other poses that engage the _____, help stimulate the Solar Plexus, increasing the flow of energy out of the vortex to the entire body.
    a. Legs
    b. Core
    c. Brain
    d. Shoulders

26. The color yellow is associated with the Solar Plexus and sight is the sense. Foods to support the health of this chakra include all except:
    a. lentils, beans, chickpeas, bananas, lemons and, pineapple
    b. ginger, cinnamon, turmeric, and cumin
    c. oranges, peaches, apricots, orange peppers, and carrots
    d. chamomile tea

27. _____ is the planet associated with this energy vortex and _____ is the element.
_____ supports and increases energy flow to the Solar Plexus Chakra.
    a. Mars, fire, heat
    b. Saturn, water, pool
    c. Neptune, ice, cold
    d. Venus, ether, space

Ésprit with SoZoKi

28. This chakra provides emotional equilibrium:
    a. Crown
    b. Third Eye
    c. Sacral
    d. Heart

29. When the Heart Chakra has diminished energy flow we experience:
    1. inhibited ability to love or be loved
    2. a positive attitude
    3. compassion for ourselves and others
    4. loss of our ability to be flexible
       a. 3 and 4
       b. 2 and 4
       c. 1 and 3
       d. 1 and 4

30. The gland that governs the Heart Chakra is the:
    a. Pituitary
    b. Adrenal
    c. Thymus
    d. Thyroid

31. Polarity for this chakra is negative, pulling energy from the Solar Plexus and pushing energy to the Throat Chakra.
   a. True
   b. False

32. Which of the following is the best choice?
   a. Heart disease is the cause of one in every four deaths.
   b. Coronary artery disease alone kills over 370,000.
   c. Prevalence of chronic obstructive pulmonary disease in 2015 was over 11 million.
   d. One in five Americans suffer from an autoimmune disease.
   e. All are correct statements.

33. _____ is the color of the Heart Chakra and the sense associated with it is _____.
   a. Gold, taste
   b. Purple, touch
   c. Green, touch
   d. Blue, smell

Ésprit with SoZoKi

34. The planet Venus rules our Heart Chakra, and the associated element is air. Scents of _____, _____, and _____, will enhance energy flow through this vortex, as well as the gemstones _____ and _____.
   a. dragon's blood; saffron and rose; coral carnelian, opal
   b. heliotrope; chamomile and rose; green tourmaline and kunzite
   c. cinnamon; rose and lavender; garnet, tourmaline
   d. none of the above

35. As energy has flowed with inspiration and intuition has been integrated, a judgement or opinion was formed and then contemplated. Next, the _____ Chakra gives rise to what we _____ to the world.
   a. Hip, Experience
   b. Crown, Practice
   c. Third Eye, Sense
   d. Throat, Communicate

36. When this chakra is closed or dysfunctional our vocalizations become negative, seeking to denounce or denigrate, rather than lift or elevate those with whom we interact.
  a. Sacral
  b. Root
  c. Third Eye
  d. Crown
  e. none of the above

37. The _____ Chakra provides the ability to see others as whole individuals. When closed or dysfunctional our vocalizations become negative, seeking to denounce or denigrate rather than lift or elevate those with whom we interact.
  a. Throat
  b. Third Eye
  c. Crown
  d. Heart

38. Speech can be used to "divide and conquer," or fracture unity through criticism, defamation, and divisiveness.
  a. True
  b. False

39. The gland that governs the Throat Chakra is the _____. In the United States, there are around 100,000 new cases of parathyroid disease diagnosed annually. The American Thyroid Associated (ATA) reports more than 12% of our population will develop _____ disease during their lifetimes.
    a. Adrenal, adrenal
    b. Parathyroid, thyroid
    c. Thyroid, thyroid
    d. Thyroid, Parathyroid

40. Anatomical connections associated with the Throat Chakra include throat, neck, ears, sinus, parathyroid and the upper respiratory system. Statista's statistics portal reported expected revenue from the sales of _____ and _____ medicines in the US to be as high as $8,977 billion in 2018 and rising rapidly.
    a. Parathyroid, thyroid
    b. Cold, cough
    c. Asthma, steroid
    d. none of the above

Ésprit with SoZoKi

41. The Throat Chakra possesses _____ or _____ tendencies and when energy is flowing freely to and through this vortex, active energy, positivity, upward-seeking, heavenly, and productive aspects arise.
    a. Masculine, yin
    b. Feminine, yang
    c. Masculine, yang

42. Diets to support the health of this chakra include adequate amounts of fluid intake to ensure your throat is lubricated. Sore or scratchy throats inhibit our natural speech-patterns, so ensure you are not mistaking a chakra issue with a simple lack of fluid intake.
    a. True
    b. False

43. Using the color blue, wear or hold turquoise, light sandalwood incense and drink Thai Butterfly Pea Tea made with organic dried blue flowers then focus your mediation on the _____ Chakra.
    a. Crown
    b. Head
    c. Heart
    d. Throat

44. The color _____ is associated with the Throat Chakra. Foods available for consumption include:
   a. Blue; blueberries, blue corn, blue potatoes, and edible flowers such as borage and blue orchids.
   b. Blue; tree fruits that naturally fall when ripe such as peaches, plums, mangos, and avocados are a great source of hydration for additional food support.
   c. Blue; blueberry smoothies, yogurt & pies or cobblers, and salads with edible flowers are appetizing ways to include a boost to your diet to benefit this energy vortex.
   d. All of the above

45. _____ is the planet associated with the Throat Chakra, and _____ is the element.
   a. Mars, fire
   b. Moon, water
   c. Earth, lead
   d. Mercury, ether

46. It is in this chakra where we come to an understanding of our place in Creation.
   a. Crown
   b. Third Eye
   c. Heart
   d. Root

47. When energy is blocked or diminished, we may find it difficult to learn new skills. Our memory and pattern recognition, which are the basis of our ability to classify data and experience, may be impaired.
    a. True
    b. False

48. What is the prime function of the Third Eye?
    a. Judging existence
    b. Integration and understanding
    c. Listening to communicate
    d. None of the above

49. Considered the center of clairvoyance. It is here that we have our sixth sense, our psychic ability and is the sense that resides within our celestial rather than physical body. The Divine principle of this chakra is the use of imagination and clairvoyance to see our spirit as it relates to all Creation.
    a. Throat
    b. Root
    c. Third Eye
    d. Crown

Ésprit with SoZoKi

50. The Third Eye regulates unconscious bodily functions such as circulation of the blood, respiration, and digestion. Anatomical connections to this energy vortex include:
    a. The brow
    b. The Eyes
    c. Hypothalamus
    d. Autonomic nervous system
    e. all of The above

51. As is the _____, the _____ Chakra is identified as having an androgynous property, the state of unified duality. Connected to both yin and yang, feminine and masculine, it embodies the surrender of each to the other. Not dominated by either extreme, the energy vortex is the same in females and males and is the seat of a melting-pot of emotions, both positive and negative.
    a. Sacral, Third Eye
    b. Root, Third Eye
    c. Crown, Third Eye
    d. Solar Plexus, Third Eye

Ésprit with SoZoKi

52. Indigo is the color of the Third Eye Chakra, the color of _____ and _____ to humanity, conveying integrity and dignity.
    a. Perceptiveness and service
    b. Objectiveness and hindrance
    c. Corruption and disservice
    d. Disgrace and disadvantage

53. What should be consumed to boost energy flow to the Third Eye Chakra?
1. Blackberries, blueberries, black currants, purple grapes, prunes, and plums
2. Apples, oranges, and bananas
3. Omega-3s is important to stave off dementia and depression, so include nuts, avocado, salmon, flaxseed and olives.
4. Dark chocolate stimulates the release of serotonin, the "feel-good" hormone, and promotes mental clarity.
    a. 1,2,4
    b. 1,3,4
    c. 2,3,4
    d. None of the above

Ésprit with SoZoKi

54. The seventh energy vortex, which completes the major chakra system, is known as the Crown, the center of _____
    a. atonement
    b. attunement
    c. enlightenment
    d. none of the above

55. The two vortices where the lines of meridian cross 21 times outside of our physical body are the
    a. Root and Sacral
    b. Head and foot
    c. Hand and foot
    d. Root and Crown

56. While the root is masculine in nature, providing positive *SoZoKi* that fires up our energy system when open and functioning, it is the exogeneity of the Crown that sustains both our physical and ethereal bodies.
    a. True
    b. False

Ésprit with SoZoKi

57. It is with a well-developed and high functioning Crown Chakra that our spirit surpasses human consciousness, and the stories we have told ourselves fade away to
    a. Self-reliance
    b. Self-actualization
    c. Self-centered
    d. Self-effacing

58. The Divine principle of the _____ is divinity in the company of higher values and wisdom. Inspiration, higher reason, and awareness are the _____ associated with the Divine's *SoZoKi*.
    a. Crown, goals
    b. Root, ideals
    c. Third Eye, facts
    d. Heart, beliefs

59. Anatomical connections to the Crown Chakra include:
1. Central nervous system
2. Cerebral cortex
3. Head and upper spine
4. Hair
    a. 1, 2, 3
    b. 2, 3, 4
    c. 1, 4
    d. 1, 2, 3, 4

60. The gland that governs this energy vortex is the _____ which is a pea-sized structure located in the middle of the brain.
   a. Pituitary
   b. Hypothalamus
   c. Pineal
   d. Parathyroid

61. When we look at life it is filled with rhythms, tide, moon, season, sleep and reproduction cycles. The function of the _____ is to release hormones that regulate sleep patterns or what is identified as circadian rhythm.
   a. Hypothalamus
   b. Pineal
   c. Thyroid
   d. Parathyroid

62. Central nervous system disorders and disease include but are not limited to
   a. Alzheimer's disease
   b. Bell's Palsy
   c. Epilepsy
   d. Parkinson's disease
   e. All of the above

63. The Alzheimer's Association reported that in 2018 an estimated 5.7 million Americans were living with the disease.
    a. True
    b. False

64. The Parkinson's Foundation reported by 2020 nearly 1 million in the US would be living with the disease and approximately 60,000 new cases will be diagnosed each year. Internationally more than 10 million have been diagnosed and are living with the disease.
    a. True
    b. False

65. There are no specific foods associated with improving or maintaining energy flow to and through the Crown Chakra because you have been consuming recommendations for the other chakras.
    a. True
    b. False

66. Although they are vastly different, the ethereal and physical bodies need _____ and _____.
    a. Socialization, contemplation
    b. Aspiration, expectation
    c. synchronicity, intuition
    d. Nutrition, exercise

Ésprit with SoZoKi

67. As you look around and see people of all ages, it is good to keep in mind that soul or spirit is on an evolutionary path. Each has something to _____ and _____ while housed in a physical body.
    a. give, take
    b. renew, support
    c. teach, learn
    d. survive, sustain

68. _____ is the planet associated with the Crown Chakra and is considered the largest ice giant in our Solar System. It was named after the Greek god Ouranos and is the only non-Roman named planet.
    a. Venus
    b. Mars
    c. Uranus
    d. Saturn

69. To clear blocks and open this chakra you will need to begin with fasting, but only if this does not interfere with the health of the body.
    a. Crown
    b. Heart
    c. Root
    d. Head

Ésprit with SoZoKi

70. _____ is the element associated with the Crown.
    a. Ether
    b. Thought
    c. Water
    d. Earth

71. To increase energy flow to and through the Crown Chakra scents include jasmine, lotus, and peony. The metal for this chakra is gold. Gemstones to work with are:
    a. Diamonds
    b. Tourmaline
    c. Clear quartz.
    d. All of the above

72. For many, the practice of a morning ritual is to sleep as long as possible before rising to:
    a. morning coffee
    b. read the paper
    c. watch the new
    d. rush of behaviors

73. Routines are a way to get things _____ but they can also make life _____, following the same steps each morning, day in and day out.
   a. considered, fascinating
   b. ignored, interesting
   c. accomplished, mundane
   d. finished, exhausting

74. If you cannot easily fall asleep, identify your evening habits that keep your mind active. Which answer below provides the best action plan to success?
   a. stop stimulating yourself a couple of hours before bed
   b. use the scent of lavender and drink chamomile tea
   c. do not read if easily engaged by a book
   d. practice meditation session and yoga poses
   e. all of the above

Ésprit with SoZoKi

75. When desiring to change perspective from half-empty to half-full, and behaviors from health ending to strength building, the time spent planning _____ _____ is essential to successful outcomes.
    a. sustainable choice
    b. your day
    c. your menu
    d. none of the above

76. When creating your intentional thought space, ensure you can freely speak to each item. You must consider everything. Of the following, which is incorrect?
    a. electricity & light control, ventilation, audio/visual capability
    b. traditional chair or comfortable beanbag
    c. space for yoga mat to pose
    d. absence of religious talismans that are important to your spiritual belief

Ésprit with SoZoKi

77. What are used to provide relief as in prayer, to maintain and sustain a community or society, to ensure knowledge is imparted and expanded through the generations?
    a. ordinances
    b. rituals
    c. policies
    d. protocols

78. In our life we eat & drink, sleep, exercise, work, play, have sex, reproduce, and create. I left out one very important thing, we_____, constantly filtering a massive onslaught of data points and variables while trying to hold on to our mind but your energy practice rituals do not need to touch on each of these aspects of your life.
    a. talk
    b. float
    c. imagine
    d. think

79. Sleep deprivation (SD) triggers negative processing of emotions which include:
    a. emotional instability and aggression
    b. anxiety and irritability
    c. thoughts of suicide
    d. all of the above

Ésprit with SoZoKi

80. Change does not occur overnight. You will need to allow and accept an honest _____. Only you, with your spiritual consciousness is involved in this process, you do not need an appointment with a therapist, nor you will not need to attend an organized group for support.
    a. conversation
    b. meditation
    c. self-evaluation
    d. none of the above

81. In the US, minimal breaks given to a work force are focused on food, drink, and restroom facilities (the body) with limited timeframe to ensure efficiency for business sustainability. Breaks are given to produce a good work product, not because the capitalist is concerned for the worker's spiritual health.
    a. True
    b. False

Ésprit with SoZoKi

82. _____ are the vocalization of a sound, a word or a series of words that are repeated when practicing meditation to bring calm and focus to the onslaught of thought that engages our mind.
   a. Poems
   b. Speeches
   c. Mantras
   d. Songs

83. While others are responsible for their behavior the same is true for you. If you wish to allow yourself to become their victim, they will lower your spirit to their human drama. If you desire to empower yourself and stop an intended or unintended assault on your spirit, then you must own your own behavior.
   a. True
   b. False

84. There is a wide variety of approach to prayer, influenced by _____, which are sometimes antagonistic. The way a person sees their world with factors including politics, culture, race, and creed influences how they pray.
   a. experiences
   b. goals
   c. perceptions
   d. desires

Ésprit with SoZoKi

85. _____ _____ are primarily used to bring energy into your ethereal body. _____ _____are associated with the upper three chakras (Throat, Third Eye, Crown) and while filled with mini chakras at the many joints they have one larger located in the center of the palm and are used to channel energy to heal another as well as bring energy for self-healing.
   a. Throat chakra, Heart chakra
   b. Feet chakras, Hand chakras
   c. Crown chakra, Third Eye Chakra
   d. Head chakras, Hip chakras

86. The first-hand position with *SoZoKi* begins with the _____ Chakra.
   a. Crown
   b. Heart
   c. Throat
   d. Root

87. Cupped hands are either touching or hovering directly over the chakras except:
   a. Heart, Crown
   b. Throat, Heart
   c. Root, Heart
   d. Third Eye, Root

Ésprit with SoZoKi

88. Hands are placed over the _____ for the Third Eye chakra.
    a. forehead
    b. ears
    c. eyes
    d. nose

89. The hand position for the Heart chakra is directly above the middle of the breastbone.
    a. True
    b. False

90. Dysfunction of the secondary chakras can have a detrimental impact on _____.
Connective tissue has a primary responsibility for carrying _____ and much of it is located in our buttocks and legs.
    a. the entire chakra system; electromagnetic energy
    b. the lower 3 chakras; impulses
    c. muscles; oxygen
    d. none of the above

Ésprit with SoZoKi

91. In our US culture, we tend to identify ourselves as _____ intellectual, giving importance to the upper part of our body over the lower part, often thinking we are a 'cut above' those with less intellect.
    a. somewhat
    b. highly
    c. a common
    d. an elite

92. Energy is pulled from the earth, but the majority of energy is brought in from _____ _____ rather than _____ _____.
    a. infinite earth, finite *SoZoKi*
    b. infinite universe, finite *SoZoKi*
    c. finite *SoZoKi*, infinite earth
    d. infinite *SoZoKi*, finite earth

93. A self-healing practice of Reiki can also open your hand chakras. The more you practice the more they will open. Resting your hands _____ while you visualize the chakras open is another opportunity readily available to most.
    a. on your head
    b. on the floor
    c. on your knees
    d. in a bowl of water

Ésprit with SoZoKi

94. A good way for you to feel energy is an exercise called 'pumping Ki or Chi'.
    a. True
    b. False

Ésprit with SoZoKi

Test Answers

1. c	11. a	21. a	31. a	41. c	51. d	61. b	71. d	81. a	91. b
2. a	12. d	22. c	32. e	42. a	52. a	62. e	72. d	82. c	92. d
3. d	13. b	23. b	33. c	43. c	53. b	63. a	73. c	83. a	93. d
4. d	14. c	24. a	34. b	44. d	54. c	64. a	74. e	84. c	94. a
5. c	15. a	25. b	35. d	45. d	55. d	65. b	75. a	85. b	
6. b	16. e	26. c	36. e	46. b	56. a	66. d	76. d	86. d	
7. c	17. c	27. a	37. a	47. a	57. b	67. c	77. b	87. c	
8. e	18. d	28. d	38. a	48. b	58. a	68. c	78. d	88. b	
9. b	19. b	29. d	39. c	49. c	59. d	69. a	79. d	89. b	
10. d	20. d	30. c	40. b	50. e	60. c	70. b	80. c	90. a	

Ésprit with SoZoKi

Glossary

Body: the physical structure and material substance of an animal or plant, living or dead
Chakra: any of the seven major energy centers in the body
Creation Energy: the act of producing from The Creator, God, available power
Creation: the act of producing or causing to exist
Creator: a person or thing that creates; The Creator, God
Divine: of or relating to a god, especially the Supreme Being
Energy: available power; a term used to describe a trait of matter and non-matter fields
Energy Vortex: available power in a whiling mass
Ethereal: light, airy, heavenly or celestial
Ethereal Energy Body: light, airy, celestial with available power to fill our physical structure
Human: of, pertaining to, characteristic of, or having the nature of people
Human Being: any individual of the genus *Homo*,

Ésprit with SoZoKi

especially a member of the species *Homo sapiens*

One: being or amounting to a single unit or individual or entire thing, item, or object rather than two or more

One Will of the Creator: a singular, determined or sure source, found in the center of all that exists

Place: a particular portion of space, whether of definite or indefinite extent

Reiki: a form of therapy in which the practitioner is believed to channel energy into the patient in order to encourage healing or restore wellbeing

SoZoKi: creation energy

The Place for Humans: the earth is our home; we are the custodians of the natural world & have a duty to protect both human civilization and the biosphere

Vortex: a whirling mass. Something regarded as drawing into its powerful current everything that surrounds it

Will: expected or required. Determined or sure

Ésprit with SoZoKi

Epilogue

When I wrote the epilogue for my first book *SoZoKi/Creation's Energy* I was living in Carmel, California and working twenty miles away at a business-minded hospital in Salinas. At the time of my writing, I had planned to spend two more years where I was, but yet again something larger than myself gave me a push. That's why I'm delighted to be in my home in the Blue Ridge Mountains of Virginia that I have missed so much. I arrived just in time for the spring bloom, a vision of Nature's beauty in every direction, and pollen in every breath. If you have never experienced, the nurse in me says you should come prepared with a strong antihistamine plan of self-defense.

The journey for this book has taken many turns before producing what you have just read. In the beginning it was directed at healthcare providers, specifically nurses, to incorporate into their practice for enhanced patient care. It then changed to a practice for the individual nurse to prevent burn-

Ésprit with SoZoKi

out, not necessarily to improve care outcomes. Of course, the natural outcome of preventing burnout would improve traditional intervention experiences for both caregiver and patient.

This was all before March of 2020 and the introduction of COVID-19 into our world. As I witnessed close up and personal in my hospital, and at a distance, watching the horrific experiences in cities across the country and around the world, the impact of the pandemic on nurses, doctors, respiratory therapists, and the many others who provided support on the news, I was spurred to focus on the individual as I developed the *SoZoKi* program. I was constantly reaching out to my healthcare friends around the country, checking in to ensure they were okay, as okay they could be. I cheered them on with little text messages. In all of those conversations, not a single friend or colleague ever suggested that I stop this new direction. Instead, to my great joy, they insisted that I let them know when I was finished so they could learn more about their energy body, and particularly how to help themselves -- and their patients -- with understanding and guidance. I share this part of the *SoZoKi* journey with you, even though you may not be a "professional" healthcare provider, because everyone with a soul would acknowledge having experienced pandemic

Ésprit with SoZoKi

stress in some manner. And this program is for all of you, for all of us, because we all have a need to improve the quality of our health and life experience.

In *Ésprit with SoZoKi* I have created the rubric you need to understand your energy body. With this manual, you can develop an awareness of your energy body that will put you in a better frame of mind throughout your day. *Ésprit with SoZoKi* should be included as a necessary skill in your checklist of activities necessary for daily living.

To supplement my written work, I have been developing web-accessible passive and interactive education sessions that will further expand your ability to draw in *Creation's Energy*. Feeling and thinking better every day is a sure sign your efforts are successfully inviting energy of the Spirit into your life. Please visit www.SoZoKi.com where you can learn more about this unique skill set, ask a question, make a suggestion, or leave a testimonial. Thank you for joining me in this extraordinary journey. It's just beginning.

Before I leave you, there is one final thank you to a couple of guys who entered my life to allow you to read my books. If not for them, I would not be typing these words on this day. Gerard Rose, Esquire /Historical Author and Tony Seton, Publisher/

Ésprit with SoZoKi

Author/Producer. I will forever have immeasurable admiration and gratitude for them. Thank you are simple words, but they come from the center of my being -- from mine to your Holy Spirits!

Ésprit with SoZoKi

Endnotes

CHAPTER 2 (Root)

1. Adaa.org. (2018). Facts & Statistics | Anxiety and Depression Association of America, ADAA. [online] Available at: https://adaa.org/about-adaa/press-room/facts-statistics [Accessed 27 Jul. 2018].

2. www.statista.com. (2018). Topic: Prostate cancer in the U.S.. [online] Available at: https://www.statista.com/topics/4379/prostate-cancer-in-the-us/ [Accessed 27 Aug. 2018].

3. Cancer.Net. (2018). Testicular Cancer -- Statistics. [online] Available at: https://www.cancer.net/cancer-types/testicular-cancer/statistics [Accessed 27 Aug. 2018].

4. Cancer.Net. (2018). Vaginal Cancer -- Statistics. [online] Available at: https://www.cancer.net/cancer-types/vaginal-cancer/statistics [Accessed 30 Aug. 2018].

CHAPTER 3 (Sacral)

5. Psychology Today. (2018). East-West Cultural Differences in Depression. [online] Available at: https://www.psychologytoday.com/us/blog/talking-apes/201711/east-west-cultural-differences-in-depression [Accessed 4 Sep. 2018].

CHAPTER 4 (Solar Plexus)

6. Hassler, K. and Jones, M. (2018). Laparoscopic Cholecystectomy. [online] Ncbi.nlm.nih.gov. Available at: https://www.ncbi.nlm.nih.gov/books/NBK448145/ [Accessed 4 Sep. 2018].

7. Cohen, E., Bolus, R., Khanna, D., Hays, R., Chang, L., Melmed, G., Khanna, P. and Spiegel, B. (2018). GERD Symptoms in the General Population: Prevalence and Severity Versus Care-Seeking Patients. [online] https://www.ncbi.nlm.nih.gov/pmc/articles/PMC4275099 [Accessed 4 Sep. 2018].

CHAPTER 5 (Heart)

8. Cdc.gov. (2018). Heart Disease Facts & Statistics | cdc.gov. [online] Available at: https://www.cdc.gov/heartdisease/facts.htm [Accessed 6 Aug. 2018].

Benjamin, E., Blaha, M., Chiuve, S., Cushman, M., Das, S., Deo, R., de Ferranti, S., Floyd, J., Fornage, M., Gillespie, C., Isasi, C., Jiménez, M., Jordan, L., Judd, S., Lackland, D., Lichtman, J., Lisabeth, L., Liu, S., Longenecker, C., Mackey, R., Matsushita, K., Mozaffarian, D., Mussolino, M., Nasir, K., Neumar, R., Palaniappan, L., Pandey, D., Thiagarajan, R., Reeves, M., Ritchey, M., Rodriguez, C., Roth, G., Rosamond, W., Sasson, C., Towfighi, A., Tsao, C., Turner, M., Virani, S., Voeks, J., Willey, J., Wilkins, J., Wu, J., Alger, H., Wong, S. and Muntner, P. (2018). Heart Disease and Stroke Statistics-2017 Update: A Report From the American Heart Association. [online] ncbi.nlm.nih.gov. Available at: https://www.ncbi.nlm.nih.gov/pmc/articles/PMC5408160/ [Accessed 6 Sep. 2018].

9. American Lung Association. (2018). How Serious Is COPD. [online] Available at: http://www.lung.org/lung-health-and-diseases/lung-disease-lookup/copd/learn-about-copd/how-serious-is-copd.html [Accessed 6 Sep. 2018].

10. US EPA. (2018). 2018 Asthma Fact Sheet | US EPA. [online] Available at:

https://www.epa.gov/asthma/2018-asthma-fact-sheet [Accessed 6 Sep. 2018].

11. WebMD. (2018). Allergy and Asthma Statistics. [online] Available at: https://www.webmd.com/allergies/allergy-statistics [Accessed 6 Sep. 2018].

12. Aarda.org. (2018). Autoimmune Disease Statistics -- AARDA. [online] Available at: https://www.aarda.org/news-information/statistics/ [Accessed 6 Sep. 2018].

13. Aarda.org. (2018). Autoimmune Disease Knowledge Base -- AARDA. [online] Available at: https://www.aarda.org/knowledge-base/ [Accessed 6 Sep. 2018].

CHAPTER 6 (Throat)

14. National Institute of Diabetes and Digestive and Kidney Diseases. (2018). Primary Hyperparathyroidism | NIDDK. [online] Available at: https://www.niddk.nih.gov/health-information/endocrine-diseases/primary-hyperparathyroidism [Accessed 11 Sep. 2018].

15. American Thyroid Association. (2018). General Information/Press Room | American Thyroid Association. [online] Available at: https://www.thyroid.org/media-main/press-room/ [Accessed 11 Sep. 2018].

16. Statista. (2018). Cold & Cough Remedies -- United States | Statista Market Forecast. [online] Available at: https://www.statista.com/outlook/18020000/109/cold-cough-remedies/united-states [Accessed 11 Sep. 2018].

17. Cdc.gov. (2018). FastStats. [online] Available at: https://www.cdc.gov/nchs/fastats/sinuses.htm [Accessed 11 Sep. 2018].

CHAPTER 7 (Third Eye)

18. Nei.nih.gov. (2018). [online] Available at: https://nei.nih.gov/sites/default/files/nei-pdfs/NEI_Eye_Disease_Statistics_Factsheet_2014_V10.pdf [Accessed 14 Sep. 2018].

19. Burch RC, e. (2018). The prevalence and burden of migraine and severe headache in the United States: updated statistics from government health surveillance studies. -- PubMed -- NCBI. [online] Ncbi.nlm.nih.gov.

Available at:
https://www.ncbi.nlm.nih.gov/pubmed/25600719
[Accessed 14 Sep. 2018].

20. Rarediseases.info.nih.gov. (2018). Genetic and Rare Diseases Information Center (GARD) -- an NCATS Program | Providing information about rare or genetic diseases. [online] Available at: https://rarediseases.info.nih.gov/diseases/2932/hypothalamic-dysfunction [Accessed 14 Sep. 2018].

CHAPTER 8 (Crown)

21. Alzheimer's Disease and Dementia. (2018). Facts and Figures. [online] Available at:
https://www.alz.org/alzheimers-dementia/facts-figures [Accessed 17 Sep. 2018].

22. Ninds.nih.gov. (2018). Bell's Palsy Fact Sheet | National Institute of Neurological Disorders and Stroke. [online] Available at:
https://www.ninds.nih.gov/Disorders/Patient-Caregiver-Education/Fact-Sheets/Bells-Palsy-Fact-Sheet [Accessed 17 Sep. 2018].

23. Cdc.gov. (2018). Stroke Information | cdc.gov. [online] Available at:

https://www.cdc.gov/stroke/index.htm [Accessed 17 Sep. 2018].

24. Parkinson's Foundation. (2018). Statistics. [online] Available at: http://parkinson.org/Understanding-Parkinsons/Causes-and-Statistics/Statistics [Accessed 17 Sep. 2018].

CHAPTER 9 (*SoZoKi* Self Practice)

25. Krause, A., Simon, E., Mander, B., Greer, S., Saletin, J., Goldstein-Piekarski, A. and Walker, M. (2017). The sleep-deprived human brain. Nature Reviews Neuroscience, [online] 18(7), pp.404-418. Available at: https://www.ncbi.nlm.nih.gov/pmc/articles/PMC6143346/ [Accessed 9 Oct. 2018].

26. Adams, Susan; Forbes Most Americans Are Unhappy At Work [https://www.forbes.com/sites/susanadams/2014/06/20/most-americans-are-unhappy-at-work/?sh=eea311a341a1]

27. www.dictionary.com. (2018). Definition of mantra | Dictionary.com. [online] Available at: https://www.dictionary.com/browse/mantra [Accessed 9 Oct. 2018].

28. En.wikipedia.org. (2018). Mantra. [online] Available at:
https://en.wikipedia.org/wiki/Mantra [Accessed 9 Oct. 2018].

29. Stevens, J., Beck, D., Staniek, S. and Baribeau, R. (2018). How To Pray the Shaman's Way | Society for Shamanic Practice. [online] Shamanicpractice.org. Available at:
https://shamanicpractice.org/article/how-to-pray-the-shamans-way-issue-3-of-4/ [Accessed 12 Oct. 2018].

30. En.wikipedia.org. (2018). Kübler-Ross model. [online] Available at:
https://en.wikipedia.org/wiki/K%C3%BCbler-Ross_model [Accessed 12 Oct. 2018].

31. En.wikipedia.org. (2018). Maslow's hierarchy of needs. [online] Available at:
https://en.wikipedia.org/wiki/Maslow%27s_hierarchy_of_needs [Accessed 12 Oct. 2018].

32. Usui, M. (2018). Mikao Usui Quote. [online] A-Z Quotes. Available at:
https://www.azquotes.com/quote/579824 [Accessed 15 Oct. 2018].

33. En.wikiquote.org. (2018). The Great Invocation --

Wikiquote. [online] Available at: https://en.wikiquote.org/wiki/The_Great_Invocation [Accessed 15 Oct. 2018].

34. The Green Shaman. (2018). White Light of Protection Prayer. [online] Available at: http://shaman.natemetz.com/white-light-of-protection-prayer/ [Accessed 15 Oct. 2018].

35. Ivanmcbeth.com. (2018). The Shamans Prayer. [online] Available at: http://www.ivanmcbeth.com/shamans_prayer.html [Accessed 15 Oct. 2018].

36. Sciencedirect.com. (2018). Meridian System -- an overview | ScienceDirect Topics. [online] Available at: https://www.sciencedirect.com/topics/medicine-and-dentistry/meridian-system [Accessed 15 Oct. 2018].

About the Author

Nancy Anna Blitz is the birth and artistic name used by the author. It is as well her legal name when her first nursing degree, Associate Degree in Nursing (ADN), was earned at a community college in Southeast Alabama, and when she was awarded "Who's Who in American Junior Colleges."

The name Nancy Blitz Ruff is the author's professional name under which she advanced her Eastern and Western educations. She first acquired formal recognition for reaching the Reiki I and II practitioner levels, before earning the Reiki Master Degree (a certification, not an academic degree). She then spent two additional years, reviewing the literature to balance Western evidence-based rationale with Eastern esoteric cultural practices.

Nancy worked in a collaborative university setting with a variety of chronic pain and chronic/acute anxiety patients, before returning to Western academia. She earned a Bachelor's and then Master's Degree of Science in Nursing at Western Governor's University while filling the role of an evening charge RN at the University of Virginia.

Ésprit with SoZoKi

Nancy has held certification (CNOR) in her specialty of surgical services, has been accepted to present at the Association of periOperative Registered Nurses (AORN) International Expo, and has written a continuing education (CE) course to assist in preventing provider burnout. Her work has taken Nancy to 23 hospitals across the United States and Hawaii. From a small rural two-room hospital to multiple large tertiary care Level I Trauma Teaching University hospitals in L.A., New Orleans, Washington D.C., and Miami, Nancy has spent 38 years observing humanity in a most vulnerable state while providing care for and comfort to both patients and colleagues.

She recently resigned her position as the Director of Perioperative Services, where she lead seven units comprised of 120 employees with the help of six managers and a department coordinator (Jamie - got you in here), who together provided surgical services to the people of the Salinas Valley of California. Change has been the one constant in Nancy's journey, and it took change to enable her to complete this manual, with all illustrations, while designing a website to help you on your journey. She returned to her home in Charlottesville, Virginia to build a program that brings awareness to those seeking to live their best life. Key players in her journey were her mother, Jenelle

Ésprit with SoZoKi

Malloy Blitz, an RN; her father Navy Lieutenant Commander Victor Edward Blitz, Sr.; her aunts Orene Goan of Enterprise, Alabama, and Billie Lyles of Chattanooga, Tennessee; her ex-husband, Dr. Mark Mosley Ruff; and still today and everyday, her son, Tyler Mosley Blitz Ruff.

Last but most certainly not least, a special THANK YOU to my best boy-friend John D'earth. John and I are full fledged members of the Mutual Admiration Association, and he has been one of the biggest cheerleaders in the past 20 years of my journey. He is the Director of Jazz Performance at the University of Virginia, and is an incredible composer and trumpeter whose music has served as the backdrop to much of the art I have created. Give him a listen, I promise all jazz lovers, you will not be disappointed!

SETON
PUBLISHING

Made in the USA
Middletown, DE
10 June 2021